FIFTY SHADES *of* JAMIE DORNAN

A Biography

Louise Ford

FIFTY SHADES *of* JAMIE DORNAN

A Biography

JOHN BLAKE

ISBN: 978 1 78418 121 5

British Library Cataloguing-in-Publication Data:

A catalogue record for this book is available from the British Library.

Design by www.envydesign.co.uk

Printed in Great Britain by CPI Group (UK) Ltd

1 3 5 7 9 10 8 6 4 2

Papers used by John Blake Publishing are natural, recyclable products made from wood grown in sustainable forests. The manufacturing processes conform to the environmental regulations of the country of origin.

CONTENTS

PREFACE

Tall, brooding and devilishly handsome with a mop of red-brown hair, Christian Grey – slowly, methodically – raps his fingers on the table. The pretty brunette sitting by his side moves uncomfortably in her seat, biting her lip seductively before flashing him the sweetest of smiles. Smoothing down his tailored designer suit, the man who has become the object of women's fantasies the whole world over glances nervously around the room.

Suddenly the room breaks into rapturous applause.

'The Actor of the Year award goes to Jamie Dornan,' a loud voice booms over a microphone.

With the broadest of grins, the smouldering actor plants an impassioned kiss on his wife Amelia's lips before jumping onto a platform to receive his golden statue.

At just thirty-one, the age when boys become men, Jamie had

achieved the unthinkable: he was a bona fide actor at last and this, his first award, was proof that the gruelling years of blood, sweat and tears had been well worth it. Undeniably, Jamie Dornan – the man now recognised as the kinky billionaire in the hotly anticipated *Fifty Shades of Grey* movie – had dreamt of this moment countless times before.

It had all started twenty years previously, in a school hall back home in Belfast, where a small, chronically shy schoolboy had climbed on stage to receive his first drama prize. He had pulled off a hilarious performance as Widow Twanky in the Christmas pantomime and, with the applause of parents, teacher and classmates ringing in his ears, little Jamie Dornan knew a Hollywood career was for him. However, what the young lad from Northern Ireland didn't know was that his path to fame and fortune would be far from easy.

To anybody in the outside world, his CV as an adult star was impressive. Dubbed 'The Golden Torso', Jamie was a hugely successful male model in his twenties, who became famous for dating actress Keira Knightley and commanding £10,000 a day as he posed for some of the world's top designers.

A music career followed but acting seemed to be his forte and he soon landed a string of high profile roles including a serial killer in the BBC series *The Fall*, an outlaw in the US historical drama *New Worlds* and the formidable Christian Grey in the *Fifty Shades of Grey* trilogy, which would seal his place in Hollywood.

However, looks can be deceiving and behind the scenes his personal life would have as many twists and turns, exhilarating highs and devastating lows, as the shows that would make him famous.

The son of a doctor, Jamie and his two sisters had what would be considered a charmed childhood, growing up in a sprawling family home in an affluent area of Belfast, attending a top school and dreaming of treading the boards like his legendary great-aunt, Hollywood actress Greer Garson. But behind the sports trophies and amateur acting triumphs, a series of personal tragedies in his teenage years threatened to throw him off course. When his mother died from cancer and four friends were killed in a road crash a year later, Jamie was forced to seek help. Then years later, and just as the ex-model was making serious strides towards Hollywood, he suffered another blow when his devoted father was diagnosed with life-threatening leukaemia.

Jamie was very aware that life was precious and, following his dad's lead, the star was determined to make the most of everything he had. Indeed, just a year after his thirtieth birthday, there was much to celebrate: not only had he been fortunate enough to land a lead role in the film adaptation of E. L. James's top-selling book, Jamie had also become a father.

His two greatest life ambitions had happened within weeks of each other; as his wife prepared to give birth, the actor had been gearing up to start filming on the *Fifty Shades* set.

While he would need some serious courage and drive to pull off both roles with aplomb, the tough times had taught Jamie that with the love and support of his devoted family he could achieve anything he wanted. And as the handsome actor stood in front of a star-studded audience at the 2014 Irish Film and

Television Awards, golden statue in hand, he had everything to thank them for, saying: 'I want to thank my beautiful family for being really beautiful. I want to thank my wife Millie for being the best thing that ever happened to me. I want to thank my baby who is four months old and she's sleeping right now upstairs, she's beautiful too. And I want to thank everyone who's ever met me and who's been nice to me I guess. Thank you all.'

As he addressed the crowd, Jamie looked every inch the beautiful Christian Grey to the legions of fans watching this special moment in his life. His lifestyle, though, couldn't be more different from that of the fictional character he plays: no swanky helicopter was waiting to whisk him away from the ceremony and no champagne on ice or team of blonde assistants was on hand to tend to his every whim. Modest to a fault, Jamie is a kind, thoughtful family man with a penchant for drinking Guinness.

He is so down to earth that he likes to tidy up before his cleaner comes round and keeps stamps in his wallet because he likes good old-fashioned letter-writing, especially to his dad.

A devoted father himself, he would rather spend the night rocking his daughter to sleep in his arms than party until dawn with the rich and famous. And not only that, he even described champagne as 'poo-flavoured sand'.

However, while Jamie Dornan's life seems as far from Christian Grey's as it can possibly get, it is certainly not black-and-white either. In fact, not only have there been many shades to Jamie's past, it has been very colourful indeed.

Chapter One

GROWING PAINS

A t first glance, you'd be forgiven for thinking that James – 'Jamie' – Dornan, born in Belfast on 1 May 1982, had something of an idyllic childhood. He did grow up in Holywood after all, even if this was a rather genteel suburb in County Down, Northern Ireland, and not the more well-known Hollywood in California.

He enjoyed a privileged upbringing and although Northern Ireland was at the centre of the IRA terrorist campaign that rampaged throughout the 1980s, Jamie knew little of it.

Growing up in a sprawling family home in the well-to-do suburbs, Jamie was the youngest of three in a well-respected family. His father Jim Dornan – a doctor and world-famous obstetrician – and mother Lorna, a 'beautiful and very glamorous' nurse, had created a picture-perfect and comfortable home for their children Liesa, Jessica and Jamie, set amongst stunning gardens and protected by impressive gates. The family were also blessed with good friends and an enviable social life, and the children benefitted from outstanding schooling.

Jamie's parents were proud of their offspring, particularly since five years of infertility at the start of their marriage meant that the pair had spent half a decade worrying about whether they might never be able to create a family of their own. During the years of failed attempts to conceive their first baby, Jim's job of delivering babies on a near daily basis felt even more poignant.

The situation reached the stage where Lorna became increasingly concerned that it would never happen and so they sought medical advice. 'I can remember being investigated which was pretty basic all those years ago but I remember hoping that it would be my problem because I could cope with it, I could get my head around it,' Jamie's father said of their years of trying, but failing, to start a family.

Luckily, just as the pair were undergoing tests to determine any underlying complications, Lorna unexpectedly fell pregnant with Jamie's oldest sister Liesa. It was a life-changing moment for both of them – even for Jim, whose professional expertise was in all things relating to babies and new mothers. 'I felt physically nauseated witnessing the pain of labour suffered by my wife Lorna,' he said, adding that his helplessness was not eased at being 'put out of the room' as per the conventional wisdom of the time. 'Even though I was an obstetrician I was told to leave the delivery room for my first child; in those days we didn't have epidurals so it was assisted delivery and sometimes the man wasn't allowed,' Jim explained.

A second daughter, Jessica, followed two years later and, four years after that, they welcomed a son into the world, who was named James following a three-generation tradition. It was love at first sight for all involved and Jamie, as he was known, was quite clearly the apple of his father's eye. 'Jamie's one of the nicest people I know […] he is essentially a very good and grounded man. He's got a great sense of humour too and is sensitive in nature. We are all immensely proud of him,' Jim once said of his famous son.

Together, they were a secure and powerful unit, since family was everything to both Jim and Lorna, despite their very different upbringings. 'Every child is a product of their parents,' Jamie's father once noted in an interview about his incredible medical career, which spanned over forty years. 'So we are coloured a lot by what happens in our youth.'

For Jamie, this couldn't have been a more accurate reflection of who he was; as the schoolboy emerged as a true all-rounder, it was obvious his family had an astonishing influence in shaping every part of his being. He was not only a keen sportsman but also a talented musician and promising actor; additionally, Jamie was kind, considerate and empathic: if someone was upset and having a hard time, the youngster would instantly show kindness. This should come as no surprise as, with so many of his immediate relatives involved in the caring professions, a compassionate nature was instilled in him very early on.

His mother Lorna, in particular, helped to pass on to her young children those very important values, even though her own childhood had been less than idyllic. Like so many women in the 1940s and 1950s who had fallen pregnant when unmarried, Lorna's biological mother had been forced to give her daughter up for adoption. Fortunately for Lorna, though, unlike thousands of children of her generation, the woman who took her on was a devoted and adoring mother who raised the young girl as her own. 'In the sixties and in my teens I went out with six different adopted girls, not that I was a philanderer, it was just very common, there were a lot of people out there who were adopted in your class at school,' Jamie's father once described. 'We all know the reason behind it, because a child born out of wedlock was seen as a terrible thing and society did put a lot of pressure on these girls to adopt. One of my sisters was adopted and yes my wife was adopted too,' he said.

Although Lorna spent much of her life not knowing who her real mother was, she eventually managed to track her down, only to discover that she had a sister, too – and in turn an aunt for Jamie. 'Lorna was incredibly close to her mother, the woman who reared her. It's not always a good idea to go and find your real mother, but in Lorna's case it worked well,' Jim added.

Professor Dornan, on the other hand, was the middle one of three children, sandwiched between two sisters. He grew up in the confines of 'the rather non-PC named' Cripples Institute in Bangor, where his accountant father was manager. Although his parents doted on their children, his upbringing was strict and religious, 'although non-sectarian I'm proud to say,' as Jim later recalled.

At school, the future doctor wasn't a high flyer but 'kept going' with his education while being something of a live wire outside the classroom. 'I did talk an awful lot and I think I have and did have Attention Deficit Disorder because I was always charging about doing one thing or another,' he recalled.

As many of his best friends lived inside the institution, a job within the caring profession seemed likely from quite early on. 'I spent my time playing with children with spina bifida or other conditions and later, as a doctor, I found it fascinating to put a diagnosis on all the different kids I had known.

'The Institute was an amazing place. It wasn't that the children's families had rejected them but rather it was felt their needs were best served in an institutionalised framework. I can only remember one child who was not happy, who said he would rather not have been born.'

Jim's parents were adamant he would make a fantastic doctor but the teenager had other ideas: he wanted to be an actor. His burning ambition to tread the boards was no doubt partly due to having a world-famous Hollywood actress in the family – and not a distant relative either. Oscar-winning beauty Greer Garson was his mother's cousin, a remarkable woman who, when Jamie's acting career took flight in the late 1990s, was referred to incorrectly in the press as his 'famous great-aunt'.

Greer was an impressive addition to the Dornan family. The strikingly beautiful red-haired star was one of the most popular Hollywood actresses of the World War II era, starring in a string of famous movies including *Goodbye, Mr. Chips* (1939), the original *Pride and Prejudice* and *Julia Misbehaves* (1948). Five-times Oscar nominated, the screen star won the Academy Award for Best Actress in 1943 for *Mrs. Miniver* and a Golden Globe in

1961 for her role as Eleanor Roosevelt in *Sunrise at Campobello*.

Born in Essex, Greer – like Jamie many years later – initially didn't intend to be an actor but chose to go to university at King's College in London to study French and eighteenth-century literature. Although she had intended to become a teacher, she began working in an advertising agency and appeared in local theatrical productions. By chance she was then spotted by American film producer Louis B. Mayer and signed to the famous MGM studios in 1937, which led to an incredible forty-year career and a new and glamorous life in the States.

She was undeniably a source of fascination to Jim and his longing to follow in her footsteps saw him apply to the top London drama school, the Royal Academy of Dramatic Art (RADA). Even though, to his immense delight, he won a much sought after place at the famous institution, Jim's parents point-blank refused to let him pursue his Hollywood dream. 'My father thought it would be good to have a son that did medicine. Not for a social thing but for him success in life was education,' he said. 'Doctors were respected people and would never be out of a job. He was a socialist and it wouldn't have been down to climbing the social ladder.'

Jim understood the decision but the lost opportunity stayed with him for many years and perhaps rubbed off a little on his son. Indeed, it was undeniable that when, some forty years later, just as Jim was retiring from the NHS, Jamie finally achieved the dream of making it as an actor, the doctor was more than proud watching from the sidelines. Jamie, who was aware of what had happened, commented, 'His parents were very strict and said, "No, you're going to medical school." He's sort of living vicariously through me now. He's a great doctor but he would have been a fine actor.'

Jim's life took a different turn and he went to Queens University in Belfast to study medicine, where he found his calling in obstetrics, the field which specialises in pregnancy, childbirth, and the post-partum care of mothers and their babies.

The young medic was fascinated and overwhelmed by the miracle of birth and even four decades later, after delivering some 6,000 babies, the feeling of wonderment never wore off. It was clearly the right decision for Jamie's father after all. 'I failed a few exams, passed a few exams – but once I found obstetrics I knew I had found something that I could really relate to, I never looked back,' Jim said.

By the time Jamie was born, his beloved father was a professor with decades of experience under his belt and affectionately known as Northern Ireland's 'baby doctor'. His career as one of the world's leading obstetricians and gynaecologists was in full swing and Jim's impressive medical reputation meant future high-ranking posts within the NHS, including Director of Fetal Medicine at the Belfast Royal Maternity Hospital and Senior Vice-President of the Royal College of Obstetricians and Gynaecologists in London.

The demands of a round-the-clock career, coupled with the responsibility of raising a young family, meant that Jim had to do some serious juggling. Keen to spend as much time with his children as possible, the devoted father would often take them on his hospital rounds on Saturday mornings. Kind and mild-mannered, Jamie was fascinated when observing his world-famous dad, whose zest for saving lives had made him well-known on the hospital circuit, as he cradled the tiny newborns who were usually a matter of a few days – if not just hours – old.

Maternity wards were certainly an unusual place for a young boy to spend his free time but Jamie adored his father, and family was everything to the Dornans. The bond between father and son was particularly strong and in later years Jamie was in awe of the doctor's ability to hold down an all-consuming and demanding job while remaining an ever-devoted parent. 'He's an astonishing man. I find him hugely impressive in pretty much every facet of his being,' Jamie admitted.

The hospital rounds benefitted Jim in that he was able to spend time with his children and also allowed Jamie to witness the miracle of life from a very tender age, meaning that the actor's caring and paternal side was shaped from boyhood. Such profound experience sparked a lifelong desire within Jim's only son to have children of his own. While many men would be shy to admit it, Jamie knew from a very young age that he wanted to be a father and felt an inner confidence that it would be a positive experience. 'I get broody even when I see strangers' babies,' he confessed as a young man in his twenties. 'I've wanted to be a father for many, many years.'

Of course, he had much to draw on his own idyllic upbringing to use as a template for his own family one day. Little Jamie, being the much-loved youngest child of the Dornan brood, was immediately taken under everyone's wing. His mother taught him to read, so he became an avid bookworm, his two older sisters had a little brother to preen, protect and look after, while his father taught him all that he knew.

As a schoolboy, Jamie enjoyed all the usual pursuits of fishing, riding bikes and building camps, and his love for animals meant that his dream job at primary school was to be a ranger, which over the years grew more eccentric in design. 'I saw an episode of Lassie where there was a park ranger who drove a golf buggy. I thought it was the coolest thing. A ranger who played golf – that became the dream,' he told the *Mail on Sunday*.

Often found with his nose in a book, the youngest Dornan read as many classic childhood novels as he could get his hands on, which he later admitted was hugely influential on his path to adulthood. 'I recently reread all the classics from my youth, *Swallows and Amazons*, *Tom Sawyer* and *Peter Pan*, because they must have shaped me in an important way, but I wasn't sure how,' he commented years later.

It is true that scenes from his early childhood wouldn't have been out of place in a Hollywood movie, with long summers spent languishing in the back garden enjoying barbeques and games on the lawn, while cold Irish winters saw the family gather for sumptuous and much-loved roast dinners every Sunday afternoon.

When Jamie started school, he immediately showed an aptitude for all disciplines. His family's past – whether he knew it or not – and their rich and varied skills and natural strengths seemed to manifest themselves in the young schoolboy.

Sport was his life and he was a die-hard Manchester United fan who loved playing football. It also quickly became obvious that he was a dab hand at rugby; thanks to his speed and slight size, Jamie was ideal for a position on the wing.

He also became renowned for his regular trips to fast-food giant McDonald's to get fuelled up before matches by scoffing burgers. 'I've played on the wing since I was about eight. I've always needed to bulk up so until the modelling took off I was ramming Big Macs down my throat,' he said. 'I remember Jamie's Big Mac obsession,' a former classmate remembered. 'He was a fantastic sportsman and was the envy of a lot of his peers.'

A privileged set-up also meant that Jamie had the chance to sample more activities than many do in a lifetime; for example, he shared a passion for golf with his father, who enjoyed a weekly game. As his hometown of Holywood boasted the Royal Belfast Golf Club – the oldest in Ireland, dating back to 1881 – it was a logical step for many local residents to try their hand at the game.

As was the case for most sports Jamie undertook, he was a natural. 'I've been into golf since I was about eleven years old and now play to a thirteen handicap. I'll try anything once – yoga, Pilates, you name it, I'll give it a whirl and see what I can learn from it.'

No one within the Dornan clan was the least bit surprised by his natural sporting ability; it was in the genes after all, as he clearly took after his paternal grandfather, James. 'As a friend brought up at my [second] wedding,' his father Jim explained, 'my son Jamie was a great rugby player and my father was a great soccer player and it's amazing how sporting ability can just skip a generation. But I did enjoy rugby.'

When Jamie also showed early signs of wanting to act, those who knew the family's history once more weren't at all shocked. One of his first roles was cross-dressing Widow Twanky in his junior school's end-of-year pantomime. Although not the easiest parts for any young boy, he nonetheless performed exceptionally well. Jamie loved the buzz of being on stage and his teachers were so impressed with the performance that he was presented with his first drama award.

Excited by his success, and like his father decades previously, he suddenly became fascinated to discover that there was a famous actor in the family. His imagination piqued, Jamie decided to write a letter to Greer Garson to let her know that he was following in her well-trodden footsteps.

After contacting various relatives, the Dornans excitedly managed to track down the retired screen star to an address in Dallas, Texas. 'When you're a kid, you're not really watching things like *Mrs. Miniver* and the original *Pride and Prejudice*, so I wasn't really aware of her but I wrote her a letter,' Jamie said. 'She was living in Texas and we managed to get her address through the family. I wrote her this letter saying I was playing Widow Twanky in our primary school production – which, may I add, I won the drama prize for.'

Sadly, in April 1996, just after he had posted the letter, they noticed her obituary in the national press. She had died a week earlier from a heart attack in a Texan hospital at the age of ninety-one. 'But I promise you, that the week before we got the letter sent off it was on the news that she died. So I personally never had any contact with her. But it's amazing to be connected to her. I love watching her films. She was my grandmother's first cousin,' he explained.

Although life in Holywood was good, nearby Belfast was a sometimes frightening place to live. The rich and diverse capital of Northern Ireland, just six miles away, was at the centre of a longstanding sectarian – and violent – conflict between its Catholic and Protestant populations.

At the time of Jamie's birth, the opposing groups – republicans, whose followers believed all of Ireland should be an independent republic, and loyalists, who wanted to retain their position within the United Kingdom – were deeply involved in what would be a thirty-year conflict known as the Troubles.

Bombing, assassination and street violence formed a backdrop to life in Belfast between 1968 and 1998. At its worst, the Provisional IRA (Irish Republican Army) detonated twenty-two bombs in Belfast city centre in 1972 on what became known as 'Bloody Friday', killing eleven people. Loyalist paramilitaries, including the Ulster Volunteer Force (UVF) and the Ulster Defence Association (UDA), claimed that the killings they carried out were in retaliation for the IRA campaign, although most of their victims were Catholics with no links to the terrorist group.

Despite the fact that the Dornans were living in the leafy suburban town of Holywood, the threat of violence still remained a daily reality. Belfast was referred to as the 'European capital of terrorism' and although Jamie fortunately had little experience of the violent backlash of the Troubles, he was aware of the risk it posed. 'I come from Holywood, a lovely part of the city. Growing up there was like, "Let's go out shopping in Belfast", "no bomb scare", "ah right, f*** it". You got used to it,' he described.

Although religion played a part in his family's history, since grandparents on both sides were Methodist lay preachers, Jamie is quick to point out they were Protestants in name only. 'I'm Protestant but the word couldn't mean less to me; I just don't give a … ' he said. Explaining further, he added in another interview, 'I think people from Northern Ireland have some kind of unspoken general feeling of what it is to be around segregation. You have an awareness of it because you know how much grief it's caused. It's a tiny percentage who have ruined it for that country, that just p****s everyone else off.'

In such troubled times, the Dornans' comfortable home became in more ways than one a sanctuary from the outside world, where family came first. Additionally, Jamie was sheltered from the violence of his surroundings during his secondary education at Belfast's Methodist College, a grammar school with an esteemed reputation. The co-educational institution founded in 1865 was not only renowned in Northern Ireland for its academic excellence but also for its impressive record of achievement in music, drama and sport. Situated on the south side of Belfast, 'Methody' offered a vast array of subjects and activities to its 1,800 pupils, including an incredible choice of sports, such as golf, rowing, judo, kayaking, fencing, squash and swimming.

With all that on offer, the future model thrived, and competitive sports remained his true forte. Jamie was smart and popular, and the teenager had a close circle of contemporaries who remained friends for life.

Girlfriends, however, were thin on the ground. Against all odds, considering his future as a male supermodel, Jamie was unimpressed by his looks. He was small and slight for his age, and was constantly labelled as 'cute' by his older sisters' friends, which infuriated the rugby-playing teenager.

At the age of sixteen, he was one of the smaller boys in his class and, like his own father, he only reached his full height of six foot when he stopped growing at the age of twenty-one. The teenage years therefore were tough for someone like him, who longed to be seen as manly and sporty. And although his boyish physique didn't hinder him on the sports pitches, it left him surprisingly and disappointingly lacking in female interest. 'It's not like I cleaned up with girls,' he moaned some years later. 'I always looked young and I was very small, I hated being cute.'

He was, however, deeply interested in the opposite sex and at the age of twelve he finally managed to experience his first kiss. Sadly, it wasn't the most romantic of clinches; indeed, just like most people's first forays into romance, it was quick and not particularly memorable. 'My first kiss was that classic of behind the bike sheds at school when I was twelve or thirteen years old with a girl I can't remember,' he said.

With women out of the question at the time, he ploughed his focus into sport, music and acting. He suffered a few setbacks, and, as he was asthmatic, he had to endure the inconvenience of taking his inhaler with him everywhere he went. However, not even a lung condition could stop Jamie from prospering in competitive sport; he was focused, driven and quicker than many of his contemporaries.

He was a keen athlete who could run exceptionally fast – once recording 100 metres in 11.1 seconds. He also found himself on the rugby, football and cricket teams, and regular sports fixtures and matches meant that his devoted parents would often be seen cheering him on from the sidelines. Despite his father's busy career, Jim would try hard to make it down to the muddy sports pitch to support his son as often as possible.

However, his sporting achievements weren't accomplished without a good dose of blood and tears, as he twice ended up in hospital with a broken nose. At fifteen he was accidentally hit in the face with a ball by his tennis coach 'for cheekiness', and he ended up in hospital for a second time following a 'particularly nasty' rugby collision.

Off pitch, Jamie indulged in the rather gentler pursuit of the dramatic arts, and his enthusiasm for drama was further ignited when he joined local amateur dramatics group the Holywood Players. Run by his dad's sister, Carole Stewart, Jamie was handed a host of roles, which allowed him to practise and hone his considerable acting skills. 'I did a lot of stage stuff growing up. My auntie runs an amateur dramatic society back in Belfast so I was doing Chekhov at twelve years old,' he described. Years later, he also added, 'I loved acting and I always wanted to go to get my A Levels and go to drama school.'

His father Jim was immensely proud of the family connection and was keen, unlike his own parents, to encourage Jamie to follow his acting dream. 'My sister should really have been an actor too but in those days my parents didn't encourage it, so she's a physiotherapist but also a huge amateur dramatist. I think almost every year her productions make it into the finals of local competitions both in the UK and Ireland and she is just a star.

'Amateur drama is big in Ireland … what else do you do on a wet winter's night in Ireland or for that matter on a wet summer's night in Ireland?!' he explained.

Jamie was also a rising star in Methodist College's impressive school productions. 'He was very modest and one of his best subjects was drama,' Jamie's former vice-principal, Norma Gallagher, recalled. 'I remember him making a very good milkman in *Blood Brothers* and Baby Face in *Bugsy Malone*.' The latter was a role that had clearly been assigned to the pint-sized Jamie because of his young, boyish looks, similar to those of the fresh-faced Hollywood star Dexter Fletcher, who played the part in the famous musical gangster film in 1976.

Life was going extremely well for Jamie; apart from the usual highs and lows of being a teenager, he was happy, secure and doing well at school, with two loving parents who had been there for him every step of the way. But to his horror, everything was set to change suddenly. The comfortable world he had known and cherished for the previous fifteen years was to be seemingly destroyed in one crushing blow when unexpectedly his mother Lorna was diagnosed with terminal cancer.

It was a bitter dose of reality for the young fifteen-year-old to bear, and the eighteen months that followed were to be the most horrendous of his life.

Chapter Two

LOSING A MOTHER

'My mum was extremely glamorous, beautiful and very into style and fashion,' Jamie said at the height of his modelling career. 'Mum would have loved all this. She would have been the proudest.' Clearly, even years after his devastating loss, Jamie was still reeling from her death; Lorna was a mother who had been, and would have continued to be, fiercely supportive of everything her gifted son did. He missed her deeply.

Indeed, nothing could have prepared the Dornans for the shock of discovering that fifty-year-old Lorna had cancer. It seemed inconceivable that the former nurse, who was young and energetic, and always showed such zest for life, could be all of a sudden struck down with the disease. Just a few days before the terrible news came, Jamie's parents had returned from a relaxing weekend in Madrid with the Ulster Obstetrics Society. As she didn't feel well, she decided to go to the doctor, who diagnosed painless jaundice: a condition which manifests itself with a range of symptoms including weight loss, yellowing of the skin and loss of appetite. However, a few days later, following further tests, Lorna was delivered the devastating news that she had pancreatic cancer. And that was not all: the disease was advanced and terminal, meaning that no amount of surgery or chemotherapy could cure her.

Lorna had to face the horrendous fact that she had little more than a year to live. It seemed particularly cruel that the devoted mother-of-three, who had guided her children expertly through their formative years and seen them blossom into well-rounded teenagers, would never get to enjoy witnessing the next steps of their lives: careers, marriage and children of their own.

Jamie, along with his two sisters, Liesa and Jessica, were floored by the news. The wretchedness of the situation was even harder to bear for their father, as his years of medical training were essentially useless in this situation when he needed them the most. There was no cure and nothing that he – or anyone – could do. 'That was the most frustrating thing – knowing there was nothing that could be done,' Jim told the *Belfast Telegraph*. 'The first three weeks of her illness were incredible – the whole family was totally devastated.'

Once the shock had worn off, like so many families hit by cancer, they had to somehow get on with life. The Dornans had always been a tight-knit unit and now more than ever they had to pull together and face Lorna's cancer head-on. Jim was straight with the three children and explained that although their mother would die from her illness, they could rely on him for strength and guidance. Friends and family members also rallied round to help, including Jim's mother, who was on hand to look after Jamie and his two sisters.

'I initially didn't cope with my loss of Lorna,' Jim said. 'Myself and the kids were just devastated by it, I also had my own father who died of cancer so I had some realisation in my own backyard of what was going to happen.

'My mother had dealt with it tremendously and she was actually very helpful to me when it came to Lorna but you can't prepare yourself for that, it was totally and utterly and completely devastating for us all for quite a short period of time.

'But I've always felt I love challenges and I love finding a way around something, and I do say, "Right, we are who we are, now how are we going to deal with this?" With the kids' help and my helping them and help from the family we managed to deal with it and Lorna was great!'

Ultimately, the only way forward was for everyone to accept her terminal prognosis. Jamie coped by not wasting time waiting for a miracle or hunting for a way of saving her; instead, the young lad spent every free moment savouring the time he had left with his mother.

Although it had been distressing to hear, Jamie was also thankful to his father for telling him the truth, which meant that they could fully focus on being together for her last eighteen months and making every minute count.

Nevertheless, it was a very bleak time in his life and one he doesn't like to revisit often. 'It was a bizarre and huge, awful turning point in my life. The comfort was knowing that it was inoperable – knowing what the outcome was going to be rather than clinging on to some kind of hope that she was going to be with us. We had a year and half,' Jamie recalled.

Incredibly, despite knowing that she didn't have long to live, Lorna showed unimaginable strength for her children, and managed to stay positive and interested in the people she was going to leave behind. 'She wasn't happy all the time or anything but she didn't make it difficult for us,' Jim explained. 'There's no doubt that everybody has to have hope and the whole family and our friends did have hope but it was hope tinged with a major dose of realism.

'And, of course, it was important the kids had hope so that whatever time left was positive but I also had to be realistic with them about something that I knew was inevitable.

'But she was amazing throughout her illness and remained a wonderful mother to the end.'

Lorna made good use of the time she had left and decided that there were areas in her life that needed closure, which in turn brought some truly happy and cherished moments for Jamie. Having been adopted at birth, she decided to track down her biological parents and in doing so discovered that she had a sister. There was much to be celebrated and Jamie, along with the rest of the Dornan clan, was delighted to see his mum enjoy some very special days in her final months. 'My wife did look for her parents, we knew the doctor who delivered her and he helped her. But she did find them just shortly before her sad demise at the age of fifty and that was a wonderful experience,' Jamie's father said. 'She has a sister and she did keep in contact with her too.'

Lorna also turned to religion and was baptised. Although Jamie didn't share her beliefs, he understood why she felt comforted in turning to God. 'I struggle with the whole religious idea myself,' he told the *Evening Standard* newspaper, 'but my mother found faith again when she was dying and I totally respect that.'

In that time she also wrote a booklet which was to be handed out at her funeral; this helped her – and in turn her loved ones – come to terms with her death.

Lorna died the day after Liesa's twenty-first birthday, a year-and-a-half after her diagnosis. Despite witnessing his mother's slow demise, it still came as a shock to Jamie. The reality of living without a mother, who had been a devoted parent right to the end even when facing her own mortality, was heartbreaking. 'There's no easy time to lose a parent but it's a very transitional time being that age and a very impressionable time. It was horrific,' he told the *Daily Telegraph*. 'Going through that certainly has had an effect on the darker side of my psyche. I was sixteen …'

The experience was so frightening that Jamie could often draw on the still-raw feelings if an acting role required it. 'I'm not saying that experiencing loss is why I can cope with darker worlds, I'm not saying that for a second, but I think it opens up a side of you in terms of work that wouldn't be as accessible had that stuff not happened,' he explained.

Such overwhelming grief, particularly when his teenage friends couldn't relate to his life-changing experience, was hard. The sensitive teenager needed an outlet and confided his innermost thoughts to a diary, trying to make sense of what had happened.

Soon after suffering such a huge loss, Jamie had to go through another major upheaval, as he was sent to board for his final two years at school. It meant swapping the confines of his once happy family home, with all the memories of his mother around him, for communal living with his classmates. 'We felt that it would be better for me, I guess,' he remembered years later.

Worse still, and in a move that would be challenging for any child to accept, less than a year after his mum's death, his father had fallen in love again. A doctor pal had set Jim up with a beautiful trainee obstetrician from Pakistan called Samina. Despite there being a considerable age gap of 'about two decades', the couple fell deeply in love. 'I met Samina through a gynaecologist friend and he knew Lorna very well and he knew us all very well. He had a young registrar and he knew that I'd quite like to meet her,' Jim recalled. He described the events further: 'I was giving a lecture in Dublin and he sent her along to the conference and she came up to speak to me afterwards. It was pretty instant, for me anyway, because she is beautiful but she's also very witty, very humorous and it was her sense of humour that made me fall in love with her. I fell for her, I wooed her, I drove all the way down to Limerick to take her out for dinner.'

It was clear that his father had fallen hard for this younger woman and it wasn't long before Jamie and his sisters were being introduced to the new lady in his life. Although they – and their mother – always knew that Jim would move on after his wife's death, the three siblings initially struggled to accept the pretty medic into the fold. 'My kids have been great, though no one would say it was easy at the start,' Jim said some years later. 'They knew it was going to happen – they just did not know when it would happen and who it would be.

'But Samina and they do get on and, with hard work on all sides, we have got to the situation we are in now. Samina would be more of a friend to the girls and perhaps takes more of a maternal role with Jamie.'

Jamie's acceptance of Samina into their family, while undeniably tricky to begin with, was worth it in the long run, as marriage followed just two years later. Jim had found a new lease of life and it was a relief for his children to see their father happy again. Samina brought laughter and fun into the luxurious house in Cultra, in County Down, that had once been home to Lorna and Jim. Stepmother Samina even oversaw a revamp of the family home a few years later, a true testament to Jamie and his sisters' fondness for the new woman in their lives. 'The house had, as all houses do after a couple of decades, got a bit tired,' explained Professor Dornan in 2005 to the *Belfast Telegraph*. 'I'd already started to change it and now, under Samina's influence, it has been dramatically changed.'

It was clearly a relationship founded on deep understanding and kindness, and Samina insisted that there were no off-limit topics of conversations – their late mother would never be forgotten. 'I do talk to Samina about Lorna and, of course, many in our circle of friends knew Lorna and mention her, too,' Jim explained, adding, 'Samina doesn't mind that at all.'

While Lorna lived on in their memories and conversations, sixteen-year-old Jamie still felt his mum's absence keenly. As anyone who has experienced a bereavement will know, the overwhelming feelings of loss can grab you at any time, but as the months passed and grief was slowly replaced with hope, Jamie started to find enjoyment in life again. However, just as he was regaining strength, overwhelming tragedy struck once again.

One year and two weeks after the death of his mother, in August 1999, a group of his friends were killed in a car crash. Like Jamie, all four boys had been keen sportsmen and they had all played together in various rugby and hockey teams at Methodist College. The four pals had excitedly left school on a Friday afternoon for a weekend break at one of the boys' holiday homes across the border in Ireland. Sadly, not long into the trip, their Vaxuhall Nova was involved in a head-on collision, spinning out of control and killing three of them instantly. Tragically, the fourth boy, seventeen-year-old Chris Hanna, was alive at the scene but died later in hospital in nearby Letterkenny.

As their devastated parents were called in to identify their bodies, it emerged that the other car involved in the crash contained two sisters and their five children, one of whom – a nine-year-old boy – later passed away.

Jamie along with his fellow pupils at Methody were collected together and told the horrendous news about their classmates. The headteacher Wilfred Mulryne told the press at the time that everybody within the highly regarded school was in mourning, adding, 'It's unbelievable to imagine four boys losing their lives in this way.'

'It was a totally hideous life-changing circumstance once again that you carry every day I guess and that's not going to change,' Jamie described. 'These are events that form your identity, I think. Probably nothing too positive, I think it's changed my view on mortality and death.'

The news hit Jamie particularly hard, since he suddenly found himself grieving for five people; also, such a sudden and tragic loss would have undeniably stirred up still-raw feelings about his mum. He couldn't cope. Those around him were worried about his state of mind and he was given a counsellor to try and work through his emotions. Jamie is not ashamed to admit that he couldn't have struggled through his remaining few years at school without therapy and, looking back, he now realises that he was in a very bad way psychologically. Rereading his journals of the time, it was clear he had some very dark and disturbing thoughts. 'I don't keep a diary anymore,' he admitted a few years later, 'because I used to scare myself when I reread it. You just learn stuff about yourself that maybe you don't really need to know.'

Even after years of counselling, he is confused about the impact such major and traumatic events had on shaping his personality. On the one hand, they gave Jamie perspective, making him more able to deal with difficult situations. Losing out on a fashion contract would have been disappointing, for instance, but he could recognise that it wasn't a matter of life or death. He was well aware that his existence was precious and petty things weren't worth getting stressed about.

On the other hand, Jamie felt that it was a trauma that he could have done without at such an extremely vulnerable age, particularly since many of his friends seemed to escape such misery during their teenage years. 'I had a terrible time when I was sixteen, seventeen. Therapy got me through that – I'm not sure how I would have coped without it. It's awful to say this but it's almost better that I went through this early on because it prepared me for situations that might arise in later life […] actually I don't know that it did. It's just some s**t happened.'

Good friends also helped with his recovery, as did music, which had become a big part of his life. Jamie was an accomplished guitarist and he found that losing himself in songwriting helped him through some very dark days.

He also formed a close bond with school pal David Alexander, who not only shared his passion for music but had lost a parent too, in his second year of sixth form. David's father had died when he was seventeen, and the two boys found rifling through his record collection – which included albums by Bob Dylan, Buddy Holly and the Rolling Stones – not just therapeutic but also influential in singing and writing songs together.

The pair spent hours composing in their bedrooms and, once they had a few tracks down, they recorded them onto a CD. Enthused with their hard work, the music-loving pair decided to become a two-piece band officially, calling themselves Sons of Jim – after their fathers, who shared the same name. 'Dave and I went to school together and became quite friendly in the sixth year. We shared a lot of the same musical interests. We recorded some stuff together back in Ireland just to put on CD really,' Jamie said. As well as singing and playing the guitar Jamie also played the harmonica, which helped to shape their folk band sound.

'[Having both lost a parent] it's helpful in our song writing,' David said of their mutual understanding and shared moments of grief. 'The two of us have come up on the same street. I think we can talk about it to each other and we know what the other one is getting at when certain emotions or things are put down in songs.'

Nights out with his friends, many of whom ended up being lawyers or barristers, 'not that you'd ever know it', also helped with the healing process. And so did Sunday lunches back home with Liesa and Jessica, who were making great strides towards their future careers as marketing director of Ulster Linens and fashion designer at Diesel Ireland respectively.

Therapy also came in the guise of exercise for Jamie, as his hours of rugby and football training also started to have a positive effect on his body. The toned physique, which was later to be adored by millions of women the world over, started to emerge and Jamie began to develop into an extremely handsome young man. Much to his relief, he was no longer the small, baby-faced boy in his class. 'Because I used to play a lot of sport I've always been in decent enough shape. When I used to get asked to do a bit of body work before a photo shoot I'd lie and say, "Yeah, I'm going to the gym" but I literally never did anything,' Jamie confessed once, when discussing his muscular frame.

Even though competitive sports kept him looking well-defined, Jamie continued to be disappointed with his appearance until he was old enough to grow a beard. As soon as hormones permitted it, he grew as much facial hair as possible and felt comfortable in his skin for the first time in his life. For starters it hid his youthful features and meant that he was less likely to be referred to as 'cute' by women.

While it had 'dangerously bushy ambitions' according to the star, Jamie kept his beard neatly groomed and in later years admitted that when acting required him to shave it off, he became 'seriously humpy'. 'I think photographers and directors realise that my face doesn't quite work without a beard. I look too young to sell clothes, too young to be a dad. Too young for anything [...] I'm still fighting the cute thing. I'm definitely not happy without a beard,' he said.

While many teenage boys will identify with young Jamie's obsession with growing facial hair, even as a grown man in his twenties, the model was often gripped by bouts of beard envy. In one instance the young model was mesmerised by the facial forest of a commuter on London's Underground. 'This man's beard was massive,' he remembered, 'and I was just staring at it, I loved how it owned his face.'

With all these teenage hormones flying around, and the stress of losing his mother and a group of good friends, Jamie would have been forgiven for flunking out of school. However, against the odds and despite an incredibly disruptive couple of years, he left Methodist College with three A levels in Classics, English and History of Art. Much to his father's delight, Jamie also won a place at Teesside University to study marketing. It certainly wasn't going to take him to Hollywood but, as he was not exactly sure what path to take at that point in his life, the three-year course seemed as good an option as any.

Jamie had measured his family ties against a desire to leave Belfast from an early age, and it was time to go. He adored the city and everything it had to offer: culture, art galleries, museums, bars, music venues. Undoubtedly, for a boy like him who was seemingly interested in everything, it was a haven. 'It's a brilliant place, with brilliant people. We have our problems but it's a tiny percentage. There's a real sense of fun, a real good-naturedness – people don't take themselves too seriously. I try not to take myself too seriously.'

Going to university would also provide him with the chance to leave the comfortable environs of home to build his own life and meet new friends who knew nothing of his past, which seemed appealing – and he felt more than ready for that.

However, on arriving at Teeside, in Middlesbrough, it quickly became clear that he'd made a terrible mistake. 'Obviously his life has been coloured by the deaths of his mother and his friends and I think it has left him with a great sense of comradeship,' his father explained. 'All of it has made him very thoughtful about life in general and about what he wants to do.'

Whether he'd been derailed by recent events or he realised that a career in marketing wasn't for him, Jamie pulled himself out of university before the academic year was out and returned to Holywood to review his options.

Not wanting to rest on his laurels and desperate to stay in shape, Jamie continued playing rugby and it was then that he was picked up by the Belfast Harlequins – a dream come true. Being a star player for his home city's team was exactly what Jamie had long aspired to and everything seemed to be falling into place.

Not long after that though, in 2001, his older sister Liesa noticed an unusual advert in the local paper. Jamie's two sisters had long been adamant that their younger brother possessed all the good looks of any catwalk model so when they saw that Channel 4's *Model Behaviour* show was holding auditions in Belfast, they encouraged him to try it out.

Produced by Princess Productions, the show was similar in format to ITV1's *Popstars*; it followed the fortunes of several hopefuls as they lived together and battled it out for the top prize: a modelling contract with top agency Select. 'I wasn't too keen, to be honest. It wasn't something I wanted to do,' Jamie admitted to the *Sunday Times*. 'Back then I was playing a lot of rugby, I was a bit of a lad. Male modelling didn't really seem like the next step.'

Not wanting to go to the auditions alone, Jamie managed to persuade a friend to accompany him and so the pair joined the queue of hundreds of wannabe models desperate for a taste of fame. The duo were interviewed by the TV team and sent home to wait for a phone call which would let them know whether they had been successful enough to star on the show.

Incredibly, despite his rugged good looks and Irish charm, Jamie hadn't been picked. 'We didn't get asked back the next day,' he said. 'I was on my own from there, and it worked quite well actually.'

Although the TV executives weren't exactly enamoured with the blue-eyed boy, scouts from the modelling agency, Select, did notice him and told the handsome twenty-year-old to get in touch. Jamie was at a crossroads: he had dropped out of uni, desperately wanting to be an actor and while male modelling was an option, it was an unlikely one. One thing was for certain, though: being holed up in the small town of Holywood in Northern Ireland wasn't going to contribute anything towards making it big in America's Hollywood.

His stepmother Samina noticed his ambitious streak and encouraged Jamie to go to London to seek his fortune – he was sold. One plane ride to Stansted and two train journeys later, the good-looking, well-honed youngster arrived in the capital with a bit of cash in his bank account and a vague plan of going to drama school before wangling himself some TV or theatre roles. There was also the back-up option of being a catwalk model if the acting didn't work out. 'I loved the fact that acting didn't involve getting up at seven in the morning, getting a train with a million other people, going to sit at a desk and clocking off at 5:30 pm. When I was younger I thought maybe one day I'd be involved in sport in terms of career. I was also involved in youth theatre. Then as you get a bit older and have to make decisions about roughly where you want to be and what you want to be doing, it just kind of happened,' Jamie said some years later of his acting career.

Truth to be told, though, it didn't really just happen like that and his rise to fame was not as easy as the then established star made out. Jamie would have to endure poverty-stricken living quarters, nights sobbing in the pub and the thankless task of working as a barman before getting a hint of the good times he had dreamed of – oh, and with a little help from his dad along the way.

Chapter Three

LOST IN LONDON

It was a big risk, considering that he had come nowhere near winning the Channel 4 show *Model Behaviour*, but it looked like he might have to go with his back-up plan after all. As soon as Jamie arrived in London, it was obvious he was out of his depth. Despite coming from a wealthy family, the wannabe actor was adamant that he was going to support himself, whatever the consequences. However, with no drama school offer and no proper job to speak of, the move to London started to look like a massive disaster. The first six months, in Jamie's own words, were 'rough'.

On arriving in the capital, the wide-eyed youngster rented a flat in Hackney, East London. Although now a relatively trendy part of London with millionaire loft rooms and swanky town houses, back in the late 1990s it was still an undesirable place to live, with high levels of unemployment, soaring crime rates and cheap housing.

His newly found accommodation was the polar opposite of the sprawling detached house back home in Northern Ireland, with its generous living space and a well-stocked kitchen. The flat, located on a seedy council estate, was grim and the cooking facilities were basic. Having little cash to his name, Jamie refused to splash out on essentials so furniture was sparse and provisions almost non-existent. 'For some reason, despite the fact it's so cheap, I felt like I couldn't even afford a kettle,' he admitted, 'to make tea I'd just leave the hot tap running for ages until I got it scalding.'

Just as one might expect of wannabe actors in Hollywood waiting for their first movie role, Jamie became a barman in Knightsbridge, a swanky district of the capital that is home to millionaires and socialites. Although it earned him a wage, working in a pub was soul-destroying and it soon started to look as though Jamie was losing a grip on what he'd set out to do. For starters he was knocking back pints most nights and, due to lack of exercise and poor diet, he lost a stone in weight. Speaking of his first six months in London, Jamie recalled, 'I drank too much and didn't get my act together. I worked in a pub in Knightsbridge for six months, crying every night.'

Years of playing rugby and football at school meant that he arrived in London bulked up and healthy, but a gym pass was out of the question in his current situation. 'I lost a stone, not consciously,' he explained. 'When I was playing rugby I was in the gym the whole time. In London I just didn't go to the gym as much, at all actually, so I just naturally weakened.'

Jamie had to face up to the reality that acting wasn't going to happen straightaway; Select modelling agency, however, were more than happy to give him a go. A trickle of jobs followed over a few months, consisting of catalogue work and striking cheesy poses for the pre-teen magazine market.

In 2002 he also went to Milan to try his hand at the runway, but the trip to the fashion capital turned out to be a flop. What the agency may not have known before he arrived in the stylish Italian city was that Jamie had a very unusual walk which made him wholly unsuitable for presenting clothes along a catwalk. 'I'm not very good at walking which is weird, I know, because it's one of the first things you do,' he told talk show host Graham Norton many years later, explaining how he'd always walked on his tiptoes and was 'quite bouncy'. 'When I was signed up as the face of a big fashion house and they saw me walk, opening their show on the catwalk was immediately written out of the contract […] it was that bad,' he said later.

Therefore, it looked initially like modelling wasn't Jamie's forte either and he was already disgruntled with his career choice. 'I have no interest in being a model and I don't consider myself a model,' he said a few years later. 'I went to Milan in 2002 to do runway and I didn't get any work. I just got bitten by mosquitoes.'

His father seemed pretty unimpressed with his career choice too. 'It wasn't exactly what my dad expected of me. A lot of his mates thought it was embarrassing that I was having my picture taken for money. I'd grown up playing a lot of rugby and they all probably thought it was a wee bit nancy boyish,' Jamie commented.

Jim was also taken aback by the state in which he found his son after insisting he pop over one day to watch the rugby while visiting the capital. He arrived at his modest flat in East London only to discover that Jamie had a useless black-and-white TV with a rolling picture. 'The picture kept flickering. I sat with my dad, with a cup of tea I'd made from a rusty, hot tap watching this pathetic excuse for a telly. He just looked at me and said, "Son you can't live like this," put his foot down and helped me get out of that situation.'

It was indeed hard for Jim to see his one and only son live in such squalor, particularly when he had seen him just a few years before go through such a hard time after losing his mother. Knowing that Lorna would also have wanted to see their youngest in a safer environment, Jim insisted on helping him out financially so that he could find a flat in a better area of the city.

His show of faith paid off. With his father's backing, Jamie started to work increasingly harder and heading along a path which would ultimately lead to his true calling of being an actor. Select weren't going to give up on him either and they were about to land him the contract of a lifetime. Unbeknownst to him, and just around the corner, Jamie was to enjoy a lifestyle that he never imagined possible. He was to be one of the most famous male models on the planet, jetting from Paris to London and New York for a range of high-profile campaigns which would see him spotted on billboards in far-flung places he'd never even visited.

For the time being, he had settled into a comfortable flat in

West London under the guidance of his caring father, and life was looking a lot more positive. Jamie was still desperate to be an actor but that would have to wait for a few years yet. 'I'd always wanted to act but the modelling contracts came more easily.'

Jamie's lucky break happened when he caught the eye of fashion photographer Bruce Weber. Famous for shooting brands like Versace and editorials for magazines including *Vogue*, the snapper also undertook a great deal of catalogue work for high street brands. And when Jamie posed for American store Abercrombie & Fitch in 2001, he fitted Weber's all-American aesthetic of photographing models with a rosy glow. Dressed in long-sleeved T-shirt and brown cord jacket with his soft features framed beneath brown curled locks, Jamie possessed everything that Weber loved to capture through the lens. 'I like to feature men and women who are really healthy,' he once said, admitting that young models with eating disorders upset him.

Although slight in frame, Jamie was athletic and strong, and therefore fitted the bill perfectly. His Irish charm and modesty would also have been a hit with Weber, who not long before meeting Jamie had kicked supermodel Cindy Crawford off a shoot for being rude. He had sent the 'face of Revlon' home in tears after she upset his team working on a campaign for the make-up brand. 'She was so rude to everyone, not to me, but to the whole crew, that I didn't really go for that,' he told the *Huffington Post*.

The stunning model – who was being photographed on location at a boxing gym in Los Angeles with a group of old boxers – apparently told the shoot's art director, 'Why is

Bruce photographing those old boxers when he should be photographing me? My make-up is ready.' Weber was so taken aback by her attitude that he told Crawford, who ended her contract with Revlon in 2001, to go home. 'She's the only model I ever sent back,' he added.

For Jamie, therefore, it was something of a coup to have turned Weber's head and although he didn't revel in the idea of modelling – and never really would – he was in awe of the man who could teach him everything he needed to know about the competitive and notoriously bitchy fashion industry.

Weber was down to earth and kind, and it was clear that he, in turn, was impressed by the young fresh-faced model. 'He is a total legend. I'm not sure I know much about fashion now, but I certainly didn't years ago – but I knew who he was,' Jamie told *The Scotsman*. 'We got on very well, so for the first couple of years I pretty much only worked with him, which, looking back, is kind of ridiculous and amazing. He is incredible. He is very softly spoken and so kind and a master of his craft as well.'

Jamie, meanwhile, was becoming master of his own craft, and posing and pouting for the camera came to him astonishingly easily. He was also popular with the crew, as he wasn't a diva – quite simply he didn't believe the hype and he was there to do a job. Besides, he still couldn't believe that he was good-looking enough to be paid simply for just staring down the lens of the camera.

What did make the job fun, though, was the eccentric and creative people he would meet throughout his new career. Indeed, it was on his first ever major campaign with Weber at the helm that he came across a very interesting person. Single and alone in London, a pretty young actress was about to sweep him off his feet; it was to be a major turning point in both his professional and personal life – and the humble, straightforward world he'd known for the past twenty-one years would never be the same again.

Chapter Four

KISSING KEIRA

The chemistry was unmistakable. Jamie walked onto the set of his first ever professional photo campaign on that steamy New York day in August 2003 and there stood Keira Knightley. The pair had been hired by exclusive jewellers Asprey for their new collection – he, as the hot model with chiselled good looks who was meant to be drooled over – and Keira, the Hollywood starlet touted as the next big thing.

The stunning eighteen-year-old, who already had a string of blockbusters to her name, including *Pirates of the Caribbean* and *Love Actually*, had been signed up by the royal jewellers to put some sparkle back into their fortunes after it lost £12 million the year before … and she didn't fail to dazzle. Voted the most desirable woman in Britain by *Tatler* magazine a few weeks previously, and predicted to be bigger than 'Catherine Zeta-Jones and Kate Winslet put together', Jamie would have been forgiven for expecting his campaign co-star to be something of a diva.

Thankfully, and to Jamie's surprise, the young actress was remarkably down to earth and up for a laugh. Additionally, the pretty teenager provided a welcome distraction as Jamie set foot on his first major modelling assignment which under any circumstances would be intimidating, as this campaign was a massive deal. 'As soon as Jamie walked into Select's office his career just sky rocketed. His first job was huge, the kind of contract that most wannabe models dream of landing a few years down the line. Not only was it Asprey, but it was for legend Bruce Weber.

'Jamie models effortlessly, he was incredibly natural in front of the camera from day one, there's not a hint of nerves,' an industry source revealed.

Despite his composure, the location itself – Westbury House, a sprawling, lavish mansion in Long Island, New York – was intimidating enough, let alone the team of professionals who greeted him. Bruce Weber was taking photographs while a number of famous actors and socialites had been hired for the campaign, including Oscar-winning actor Joseph Fiennes.

Jamie wasn't the only handsome male model to be employed for the job but there was something about this fresh-faced clothes horse that must have caught Keira's eye – and it was probably his laid-back attitude to the job. In reality, since Jamie went into modelling as a means of becoming an actor, right from the start he found it easy not to take the job too seriously – that and the fact that he knew he had more to offer than just a pretty face.

'I generally don't like admitting, "I'm a model." I find that a lot of people have preconceptions – they think that you're going to be dim or vain. I'm just a guy who did modelling for a job. I actually came to London to join drama school,' he said.

Keira, already an established actor, was also at the start of her career. Just out of school, the pretty star seemed happy-go-lucky and, although ambitious, she was clearly still in the mindset of just 'seeing what happens'. This particular shoot was no exception and Keira claimed the real draw of being in the advert was getting her hands on some seriously expensive jewels rather than what it would do for her already enviable profile. 'I'm such a sucker for diamonds,' she admitted in an interview during the campaign. 'They're beautiful. I'm single at the moment and happy to stay that way for a long time, but if a man were to buy me diamonds I might change my mind.'

The singleton's laid-back attitude towards dating also appealed to Jamie and, as they hung out, not only was it obvious that they physically desired each other, they were seriously hitting it off in the personality stakes too. Like Keira, chronically shy Jamie wasn't obsessed with all the trappings of fame and its red carpet appearances and showbiz parties; instead, they had a shared passion for home-made cooking, nights in with their close-knit families and shopping for nick-nacks in charity shops.

Other men may have been intimidated by Keira's beauty and status but Jamie was in his element in the 'controlled environment' that the photographer's film set afforded him and he found it easy to laugh and flirt with the actress. 'I would have way more chance with someone who is deemed to be really beautiful – like a model or an actress – than I would with a normal girl in the street,' he said later. 'When I meet girls like that it's a very controlled environment or we're working together. In the real world when you're just out with your mates in a bar I wouldn't know what to do.'

After the shoot, the pair exchanged numbers and had plenty enough in common to keep in contact. As well as swapping stories about life in the fast lane, since they were both being inundated with job offers, Jamie admitted to Keira that he held a lifelong ambition to be an actor like her. So she put Jamie in touch with her high-powered agent Lindy King at London's PFD agency, who she was sure would put him on the right track.

With everything going their way career-wise, the pair's relationship strengthened, hindered only by the fact that it was a long-distance affair. Jamie was sent to New York, where he continued to carve out his modelling career, while Keira flew back to London where she still lived with her parents in a three-bedroom terrace house in Teddington. However, she wasn't back home for long before she had landed the role of Guinevere in big-budget movie *King Arthur* and was jetting to Ireland for the start of filming.

The pair kept in contact over the phone and promised to meet up whenever possible. Those close to the couple, and Keira's parents in particular, were thrilled about the developing romance. Her TV actor father Will and playwright mother Sharman Macdonald warmed to the mild-mannered doctor's son who appeared to share their daughter's work ethic and down-to-earth nature. 'Jamie isn't interested in being in the limelight, he's not chasing Keira's fame, if anything that would put him off,' a friend told a magazine, continuing:

'When someone like Keira goes out with a guy, you always look at the boyfriend and wonder if they are in it for their own gain. Not Jamie, he is extremely successful in what he does and shy about it. They are an excellent match.'

However, not everyone was happy. When Keira broke the news to her ex-boyfriend Del Synnott in October, he was mortified. She had dumped him a few months earlier after two years together and in November the distraught twenty-five-year-old actor was rushed to hospital following a suspected overdose. A wave of gossip broke out in the media and amongst his friends that, heartbroken, he had gone on a bender which had ended in disaster, although his family hotly denied the speculation.

Keira had fallen for the *Lock Stock and Two Smoking Barrels* star in 2001 on the set of the US TV movie *Princess of Thieves* and while she had found it relatively easy to get over their split by throwing herself into work, the actor had taken it hard. 'It was different for Del,' a friend explained. 'Del is not working at the moment and had too much time to brood on the whole affair. He got really low.'

Keira evidently still had some residual feelings – or guilt – for Del and rushed to the Royal Free Hospital in Hampstead, north London, to stay with him overnight. Under such tense circumstances, Jamie's relationship with the star took a natural back seat. 'Keira was mortified when she found out what had happened to Del. She rushed to his bedside and stayed all night. When we heard he was in hospital we all assumed the worst because he has been so upset about breaking up from Keira,' a friend told the *News of the World* newspaper. 'She has insisted that she have a break from Jamie until everything is sorted out.'

Her mother Sharman was also concerned about her daughter's ex-lover and admitted, 'We are in constant touch with the Synnott family. Del is being taken care of by his family and is well.'

Jamie, meanwhile, was still in New York and was having something of his own wake-up call after discovering – to his horror – that thanks to his links to Keira he had become boldface tabloid fodder overnight. It was the first time the model's life had been thrown under the media microscope and he hated every second of it. His agents told him not to talk about Keira and to pass on any queries to them. As a result, their phones were ringing off the hook, as journalists wanted to know every detail about the new man in Keira Knightley's life, and even Jamie's family and friends were also being approached for slices of gossip.

The handsome model returned to his family home in Northern Ireland to hide from the press and spend time with his level-headed father Jim and ever-supportive family. Those who knew the carefree twenty-one-year-old were shocked by the sudden and intense public scrutiny into his life and were worried about how his fiercely private family would cope. 'We had thought the whole relationship was off,' a close family friend admitted. 'The whole matter has come as a bit of a shock to Jamie and his family. I don't think he imagined he'd be thrown into the limelight like this.'

And while Keira was denying she had ever dated Jamie,

branding the idea as 'rubbish', the model didn't appear to be doing so well at keeping schtum and mistakenly admitted to a newspaper that they were still an item. Although the media novice had followed instructions, telling a journalist that they should contact his agent if they wanted any information, he had confirmed his relationship with Keira in doing so. 'Basically my agency have said if anyone calls me I have to forward all calls onto them,' he told *The People* newspaper. Stressing he couldn't say any more about his girlfriend, he added, 'I can't. I'm really sorry I can't.'

It hadn't been the easiest start to their relationship, but after the storm of publicity died down, the pair were able to continue their romance with less distraction. 'He's great, really sweet and sexy. I'm mad about him,' she revealed. 'He keeps me sane when things get stressful and we always have fun.'

The duo discovered that they had an incredible amount in common: shunning posh eateries for small cafes and bistros, shopping in charity shops and even taking the bus over expensive cabs. 'I still get on the bus and go shopping at the supermarket,' Keira admitted in a newspaper interview, 'although with my face on just about every bus it's been a bit more difficult really.'

Jamie was also the perfect gentleman to her English rose: polite, shy, driven and, above all, loyal. Keira was dating someone who, despite his good looks, wouldn't stray. 'I'm a loyal person,' he explained. 'I hate the idea of even switching banks. Even though I could be saving money, I really like the guy at the bank, so I just couldn't let him down.'

Although they were both successful in their own right – Keira had started to command over £1.5 million a film and Jamie was being inundated with modelling requests – they both shared a desire to lead as normal a life as possible. However, with their heavy work schedules meaning that they were often thousands of miles apart, it was going to be tough. Keira had already admitted that she was finding it difficult keeping tabs on her personal life. 'I woke up one morning and realised I haven't spoken to my best friend for a month-and-a-half. She'd split up with her previous boyfriend and already got another one and I didn't know about any of it,' she said at the time. 'I'm not good with phones and I don't have email, I can't use a computer, so not being in touch is totally my fault.'

It was clearly a case of absence makes the heart grow fonder for Keira, though, when she admitted to missing Jamie on the set of *King Arthur*. After four months spent in Ireland's Wicklow Mountains filming the historical blockbuster, she was pining for more than just dinner dates with the handsome model. 'I feel like I'm at university but without the shagging – which is unfortunate,' she confessed.

As they saw each other so little, it was no surprise when the rumour mill started churning out stories in early 2004 that they had split – and by February there were whispers in the press that Jamie had lost his girlfriend to actor Adrien Brody, who was playing Keira's lover in the psychological thriller *The Jacket*.

The pair had the obligatory steamy sex scene together and Adrien was reportedly helping to calm her nerves by taking vodka and brandy to her caravan before shoots. They were also staying in the same block of flats in Glasgow and had been spotted exploring the city's nightlife together, including a 'date' at a White Stripes gig. In February 2004 news agency WENN claimed that Keira was inseparable from her handsome co-star, adding, 'This follows Knightley's recent split with model Jamie Dornan. A movie insider says, "They are very close and spend a lot of time together. Keira and Adrien really seem to have clicked."'

The rumours of an affair were false and it was the first of many trying situations that the new couple would have to face together. A furious Adrien also hit back later in the year when the stories were threatening to damage his own relationship, as well as harming Keira and Jamie's reputation. 'We were said to be having intimate, candlelit pasta dinners at my apartment, but that's not true,' he explained. 'We ate together a couple of times because we were working but it never went further than that.'

Two weeks after reports of their split, the now billboard-famous model jetted to Glasgow to see Keira on set and the pair were seen strolling through a park in the Scottish city before stopping for a hug and intimate chat. It was quite clear that the relationship hadn't quite fizzled out yet – far from it, in fact. Behind the scenes the pair had started discussing their future together and Keira – despite her promising start in acting – was considering a change of tack by going to university.

Jamie was reportedly 'dead against' her plans to go to Oxford Brookes, since he had always rejected the idea of getting a university degree in favour of choosing his own path instead. He also reportedly allayed concerns that despite her latest film *King Arthur* being panned by critics, her career was too good to give up. Cruel cynics mused, meanwhile, that he was probably worried that his famous lover would be mobbed with male students wanting to date her. 'Jamie thinks Keira is making a name for herself in Hollywood and can study anytime so doesn't understand why she wants to do it straight away,' a friend told a newspaper. 'He feels she is only eighteen and the world is her oyster. He just wants to make sure Keira makes the right decision. He seems to think she'd be completely mobbed with male admirers at university whereas in the world of film she's one of many beautiful people and less likely to be led astray,' a source added.

Once filming on *The Jacket* finished in March, it was Jamie's chance to patch things up with Keira properly. When she returned to London to celebrate her nineteenth birthday at home, he finally managed to spend some quality time with her; he also started to get to know the Knightley family and it was clear that he fitted in well. Keira's mother Sharman immediately warmed to her daughter's new beau and quickly became a confidante to Jamie, as the young showbiz couple in the coming weeks and months began to struggle with certain negative – and very frightening – aspects of fame. 'Sharman was very fond of Jamie – of all Keira's boyfriends, he is her favourite,' a family friend revealed a year later after their split. 'It may have been something to do with the fact that Jamie had lost his own mother at the age of sixteen and Sharman has been almost a surrogate mum to him recently.

'Jamie is such a vulnerable kind of guy, plus she is Scottish and he is Northern Irish and that Celtic connection may have helped them get along.'

With a break in filming, the pair had time at last to nurture their relationship and found plenty to keep them busy. Since it was Keira's birthday, she decided to go on a well-earned shopping spree and as well as looking for a car – 'a Mini Cooper S in black' – the loved-up duo were also spotted house-hunting together. It was time for the pretty actress to move out of her parents' house, and she invited Jamie to come and live with her. 'I don't know if they found anywhere suitable but Jamie certainly seemed to enjoy looking!' one onlooker noted as they browsed estate agent windows in west London.

Keira eventually snapped up a £1.5 million apartment in fashionable Mayfair and in June 2004 the pair moved in together – along with a few friends. 'I actually moved in with about six people in the end,' she told US talk show host Jay Leno, 'which was a bit of a problem because there were only two bedrooms. It was very crowded! But I kept on asking more people to move in, forgetting that I only had two bedrooms.' Far from a romantic love nest for two, the apartment also had further problems: 'It's got water pouring through the ceiling, the electricity doesn't work and the toilet broke,' she admitted at the time.

After a period of temporarily moving back to her parents' house while the issues with their new house were fixed, the pair began living together properly and Jamie got to know 'the real' Keira. Having grown up with two sisters, Jamie was used to living with girls but even so he probably hadn't bargained on Keira being something of a tomboy who liked to break down inhibitions by farting. 'As soon as you fart in front of somebody, the whole illusion has gone in an instant,' she explained.

Not put off by Keira's toilet humour, Jamie was now head over heels in love with the pretty star and evenings were spent preparing her home-cooked meals – including his specialities, roast dinners and spaghetti bolognese – while she challenged gender stereotypes by buying him flowers. However, the domesticity seemed to end there, as Keira admitted that she would often take their dirty laundry back to her mum's house in Teddington.

Family ties were strengthened further when Jamie invited Keira back to his childhood home in Northern Ireland where she was welcomed with open arms by his adoring family. Keira immediately struck up a bond with his sister Jessica, a former designer for clothing brand Diesel, over their mutual love of books and fashion. She also proved a hit with his father Jim, who clearly believed the film star was something of a positive influence on his son after the tragedies of his teenage years. 'Well, she's a very nice person indeed,' the fifty-six-year-old consultant obstetrician proudly told the *Belfast Telegraph* in late 2004. 'I've met her a few times and she's actually very straightforward. She's visited Northern Ireland and like Jamie she's a huge fan of the sandwiches you get in Doorsteps on the Lisburn Road.'

It wasn't long, therefore, before stories started to emerge that Jamie was to marry his famous girlfriend of just under a year. 'They were spotted strolling around Bond Street the other day looking in shop windows at diamond engagement rings. Keira seemed to have her eye on something pretty special and she's told friends she'd love to get married sooner rather than later,' a friend divulged to the *Daily Mirror* newspaper.

'They also visited a jeweller in Harrods but the store was sworn to secrecy and promised not to talk. It seems they are preparing to get engaged, or maybe they've already done it and kept it a secret.' Discussing the couple's previous 'rocky' relationship and the home they were now enjoying together, the source added, 'There have been a few problems with renovations at the apartment but they're settling in well.' Keen to scotch the marriage rumours, Keira broke her silence a few days later in a magazine interview, saying, 'Jamie's great but I'm way too young for marriage. One day in the future, maybe, but marriage and kids are just not on my mind at the moment.'

In fact, Jamie and Keira had more serious matters on their plate. The stunning actress now had some major films under her belt and since becoming instantly recognisable – especially as she was living in one of the most sought after districts of London – her fame was coming at a price. The more famous Keira was becoming, the less freedom they seemed to have and at times the situation was becoming disturbing. Jamie was now seriously worried about Keira's safety – and, naturally, his own by association – as she was being chased by paparazzi on a weekly and sometimes daily basis, as well as being stalked by obsessive fans. 'I have found myself thinking, "look what happened to Diana",' Keira admitted at the time, in reference to Princess Diana who had died seven years previously in a car crash during a paparazzi chase. 'For some reason your instinct is to run away and you really do begin to think, "Oh my God, there could be an accident here".'

Fans had also begun to lie in wait for Keira to return home at night and her terrified mother Sharman had started a regular ritual of combing the streets before letting her daughter out of the car in case someone jumped on her. 'This nutter has been hanging outside my house, it's been really alarming. My mother has been so upset and I just hate it,' Keira revealed.

'Keira plays it cool but you can understand her mum's worry. This bloke has really shaken Sharman up,' a friend said in 2004. 'He is probably just a harmless fan, but you can never be too sure. There are so many weirdos in London.' Jamie also shared Sharman's concerns and told BBC Radio Ulster some days later, 'She's a nineteen-year-old girl and if she goes anywhere on her own, there's men following her. It's almost certainly paparazzi but there's the off chance that it could be some absolute weirdo.

'You do get quite aware of the paparazzi and stuff, but I do think they're the lowest. I can't handle them at all.'

It was increasingly obvious from Jamie's rare openness about the situation that the responsibility of dating someone in the public eye was taking its toll. He and Keira had started to dress down when leaving the house in order to try not to draw attention, with the actress wearing baggy trousers, beanie hats and no make-up. Nights out were also being replaced with evenings in front of the TV in order to avoid being out in public. The relentless attention, however, wasn't just confined to London, as residents living close to Jamie's childhood home in Holywood, County Down, had also noticed the model's now famous girlfriend arriving in town for weekend breaks. 'She has been over before but no one really recognised who she was – it will probably be a lot harder now,' a source told the local paper. 'If she lands in Ireland you'll be the first to know.'

Matters seemed to go from bad to worse when at the London premiere of *King Arthur* the pair were at the centre of a terrifying security alert. Looking stunning on the red carpet, Keira appeared every bit the A-list celebrity as she stood dripping in £250,000-worth of diamonds on loan from Asprey's and accompanied by Jamie in a designer black silk suit and shirt. Thousands of fans had turned out to the event in Leicester Square and the young couple couldn't believe the reaction she was getting. 'I can't believe how many people are here,' Jamie's now famous lover was overheard saying. 'I don't believe I could ever get used to this sort of reaction.'

The couple were clearly bowled over by the turnout but as the evening wore on, their feelings of excitement turned to disbelief when, due to a 'breakdown in communications' with organisers of the event, the duo were left alone during a terrifying crush in the VIP area, without her security guards in sight. Worried the necklace and bracelet would be stolen in the mayhem, security staff stormed through the crowds and swooped on the actress before dramatically stripping her of the jewels from around her arm and neck. Jamie and Keira were left feeling exposed and very, very scared. 'I was really quite frightened. Security rushed in here at midnight and took them off me [...] it was terrifying to have all these people crushing around me when I was wearing all that money,' she revealed at the time. 'Now they're safely away I can just party with Jamie – he was really worried about my safety.'

Being plunged headlong into the world of celebrity was without doubt beginning to become something of an arduous task for Jamie, as he tried hard to enjoy his own 'normal' life, which he prized so much. It was, after all, not his career that was bringing the international fame and intrusive attention, but Keira's. Being her partner required a massive dose of responsibility and loyalty – it was undoubtedly a big ask. While she took centre stage publicly and reaped the financial rewards, he was forced to take something of a back seat, despite the fact that he was being scrutinised almost as much.

Back home in Ireland, his every move was being documented and celebrated – it was now something he couldn't escape. 'The image of Ulster males got a makeover last week when twenty-one-year-old Holywood model, Jamie Dornan appeared arm-in-arm with hot actress Keira Knightley at the world premiere of her new film, *King Arthur*,' his local paper proclaimed. 'The stunning actress had Jamie as her escort and most of the world's paparazzi flashbulbs were popping in the direction of the good-looking young couple, propelling the Co Down man onto the international stage.

'With his easy style, cropped blond hair, tanned skin, grey-blue eyes and natural stubble, Jamie is the epitome of relaxed glamour – a real Holywood man – Holywood, Co Down that is.'

Keira, meanwhile, was making headlines in glossy magazines and newspapers the world over; photographers were trailing her wherever she went and with every film came relentless TV and press interviews, and red carpet appearances. Jamie, as dutiful boyfriend, was now expected to behave impeccably so as not to damage her reputation, remaining tight-lipped about the intricacies of their relationship while at the same time enduring the various security threats that now engulfed them as a couple. 'She's the most beautifully grounded person I've ever met,' Jamie said a year later. 'It's very scary walking down the red carpets. And unless you're the kind of person who likes answering questions about who made your dress – which Keira isn't – you're scared. Keira is just a young girl.'

It wasn't going to be easy but for now, at least, Jamie appeared to be happy and very much in love, and they were facing this crazy world of showbiz together. 'You would wake up and read the papers or look online and see a photo of Jamie with Keira coming out of somewhere like Pret a Manger,' a source close to the couple admitted.

'According to the columnist, he enjoyed a "tuna mayonnaise and rocket" sandwich that day,' the source continued. 'It was completely bonkers, you couldn't make it up – the world knew more about him than his mates. You did question how long someone as private as Jamie would be able to put up with that level of intrusion. To be fair, he seemed fine with it, so no one was going to question it. Keira was obviously worth the hassle.'

Chapter Five

IN IT FOR THE LONG HAUL

There was no doubt about it: Jamie was smitten.

Keira's career had now taken her to Hollywood, where she was filming action thriller *Domino*, and it wasn't long before the proud model was jetting to Los Angeles to take his famous girlfriend Christmas shopping. The couple were already dodging nasty rumours that Jamie was only in it for a career leg-up but the truth was that they were a young couple in love. 'He keeps her sane,' a friend of the pair said at the time. 'Keira's the first person to admit that. He's so down to earth and sweet, it would be all too easy for Keira to be consumed by her career but he reminds her that there's a world outside Hollywood.'

Strolling hand in hand through Tinseltown, the couple were seen diving in and out of shops, emerging from a bookstore with a Bob Dylan autobiography before stopping at underwear boutique Victoria's Secret. It was clear their relationship was flourishing despite the need for them to travel great distances – sometimes thousands of miles – to spend time with each other.

In January 2005, ever understanding of Keira's career, the handsome model was snapped by her side at the Sundance Film Festival in Utah to watch a screening of her film, *The Jacket*. A month later they were reunited in London, this time huddled in each other's arms while walking around the antique stores of Notting Hill in the rain. 'Keira had a spring in her step, she was walking hand in hand with Jamie and you can tell they are totally loved up,' an onlooker noted to a magazine at the time.

The pair had returned to the capital for Keira's twentieth birthday, which was to be a modest affair with just close friends and family. 'I like to go to normal places – just basic bistros and cafes,' she admitted. 'I've never been the kind of person to go out to places like The Ivy and pose, it's just not me.'

The truth was, of course, that it was becoming impossible for Jamie and Keira to meet in public places, even if they wanted to. Keira had worked on three film sets in 2004 and the media interest was overwhelming; when she wasn't being hounded for a press or TV interview, there was another premiere to go to, a charity event to attend or auditions and rehearsals for the next role.

It wasn't like Jamie was waiting in the wings either; his modelling career was seriously taking flight and endless bookings were now taking him across the globe. Ever since the Asprey photo shoot with Keira, Select had been inundated with requests for fresh-faced Jamie to grace their campaigns. The buzz surrounding his relationship had undeniably helped and, after escorting his famous girlfriend down the red carpet at the New York premiere of *King Arthur* in June 2004, his international profile had soared.

It wasn't long before he was fronting an advertising campaign for Calvin Klein. It was the major modelling breakthrough he'd been waiting for. In a series of controversial, erotic shots for the designer's autumn 2004 range, Jamie appeared writhing on a beach with Russian supermodel Natalia Vodianova in skintight black jeans and with a rippling, bare torso.

So successful was the campaign that he became a firm favourite with the fashion house overnight, and future jobs were sent his way when the CK group booked him two seasons later – this time opposite the formidable supermodel Kate Moss. The snaps also proved to make him something of an ambassador of the Calvin Klein lifestyle, a brand which was described in the press as 'hot, sexually provocative and steamy' and deemed so 'pornographic' in some quarters that they provoked demonstrations beneath billboards.

Behind closed doors, though, Jamie appeared nonplussed with the fuss that the sexy adverts fuelled. 'Calvin Klein wants to be controversial, so if people are demonstrating under a billboard of me getting my arse bitten by Natalia Vodianova, then that's a win for them, because it creates attention,' he told *The Times* newspaper. 'I hope that's the closest I'll ever come to porn.'

Throughout the summer more signings came, with Jamie fronting collections for Tommy Hilfiger and British designer John Richmond. 'Jamie Dornan is one of the most exciting new faces to hit the international model scene this year,' *Showcase* magazine wrote in June 2005, alongside a photo of Jamie with a shaved head and modelling a John Richmond T-shirt.

Now living in New York, the offers were coming in thick and fast, and the year heralded a Caribbean-inspired print campaign for Armani Exchange and a photo editorial in *GQ* magazine, in which Jamie was heralded as 'the male Kate Moss'. 'In the span of twenty years, I've seen maybe four models who have what Jamie Dornan has,' said Jim Moore, the long-time creative director at *GQ*, who put much of his success down to having a face the camera loved. 'There is something else though. He's like the male Kate Moss. His proportions are a little off. He has a slight build. He's on the small side for male models. But his torso is long, and so he looks taller, and he brings a relaxed quality to modelling. He knows what he's there for, but unlike a lot of people he's not trying to be a male model. He is not modelling.'

Astonishingly, and in typical Jamie fashion, he didn't believe the hype. Instead, he was attributing his newfound success to American bookers being fooled by his Irish charm. 'I think the only reason I've done well to date is that I don't take it very seriously,' he told a local radio station in Northern Ireland. 'I feel completely blessed to be able to do it, and it's a great way to make money, travel around and have a laugh.

'[…] You go over to America, talk to some people in an Irish accent, and they love it. They think you're all very nice, and they book you.'

The shoot for men's magazine *GQ* in January 2005 was a roaring success, with their website inundated with comments from adoring fans – both male and female. Ironically, the shot – which saw the Irish star posing in a charcoal grey suit with his hair slicked back – was pulled out of the archives in 2013 by *E! Online* and posted on its website in the wake of Jamie's casting in *Fifty Shades of Grey*. 'Even though Jamie is fully clothed in *GQ*'s January 2005 issue, he still embodies all the sexiness that is Christian Grey even back then,' a journalist on the entertainment website swooned.

It was true to say that 'even back then' – in his twenties – it was abundantly obvious that this young model had something out of the ordinary. Indeed, it was no surprise then that news of his ability to act so effortlessly for the camera had started to spread throughout the industry and the first mutterings of Jamie being touted as an actor started to emerge. A friend admitted a few weeks after the *GQ* editorial that Jamie was being put forward for screen parts. 'Jamie is modelling with Select but he's been approached by a number of leading acting agencies. He's Irish, dark-haired and can grow great facial hair so he's being touted as the next Colin Farrell,' the source told Britain's *Mail on Sunday* newspaper.

Until that moment, Jamie's life had been focused on two things: modelling and Keira. As his career was about to crank up a gear and perhaps follow a new path into acting, the love-struck pair decided to seize on a quiet break in their schedules in April to take their first holiday together. Packing their bags, they jetted to a luxury resort in the Caribbean, where they hoped to enjoy the golden sands and crystal clear pools far away from the Hollywood limelight. Eager to keep his girlfriend happy,

Jamie also went to amazing lengths to ensure that Keira had a romantic break to remember at their sumptuous hotel in St Vincent. 'Jamie ordered hotel staff to cover their bedroom in rose petals and light fifty candles. He wanted to give her a really romantic night – and it's fair to say she was impressed,' a source told *The Mirror* newspaper.

But this such precious 'alone time' the pair so desperately desired was short-lived and within hours of touching down in the tropical paradise, the paparazzi were hot on their heels. A day later the first ever photos of Keira in her bikini were splashed across newspapers back at home in the UK.

The chaos didn't stop when they returned to work, and it was becoming increasingly clear to Jamie's friends and family that as well as the endless press intrusion, his busy schedule was also starting to suffocate their relationship. Keira was quite clearly in love with Jamie but her greatest passion remained her career. She was now working flat out; with the role of Elizabeth in Jane Austin's classic *Pride and Prejudice* under her belt, she had signed up for not one but two sequels to *Pirates of the Caribbean*, playing opposite Hollywood legend Johnny Depp. It was revealed that she had been paid a staggering US$12.6 million to reprise her role of Elizabeth Swann and, along with the rest of the crew, she was now deeply embedded on set for the best part of the next year. Keira's professional life had been moving incredibly fast, placing enormous strain on their long-distance relationship but it wasn't her career that was going to push them further apart – it was his.

Thanks to the agents Keira had signed him up with, the

rumours were indeed true: Jamie was finally about to realise his childhood dream of being an actor. He had landed his first film role in Sofia Coppola's film *Marie Antoinette*. The call had seemingly come out of the blue – one minute Jamie was rehearsing with his band, Sons of Jim, at his London flat and the next his agent was telling him that film director Sofia had been on the phone asking if he was free to star in her latest movie.

She had apparently heard about Jamie from a photographer friend in New York, who was convinced that he had all the credentials to become a film star. Astonished by the remarkable offer, Jamie flew to Paris immediately for an afternoon audition and the following day was told he had got the part. The square-jawed model was to play opposite *Spiderman* beauty Kirsten Dunst, as the queen's lover, Axel von Fersen. It wasn't a massive role by any means but Jamie was over the moon that his talent had finally been noticed.

Despite being deeply grateful for the chance to prove himself on screen, he was clearly suspicious of the quick casting and was convinced that he had only landed the part because they couldn't find anyone better. 'It was the last role cast. I guess there had been pressure to have a certain ilk of actor, some big name from the up-and-coming list, but they hadn't been able to find someone.'

Although Jamie was dogged with self-doubt, Coppola and the movie's production team immediately saw he was more than just a pretty face and believed they had found a talented actor in the making. 'We were very impressed by Jamie's audition, he definitely has an untapped talent there,' a production source told the *Daily Mirror* newspaper. 'Without giving the movie away to those who don't know the story, Jamie's character Hans is an admirer of Marie Antoinette and spends much of the film having his love unrequited.'

Down to earth and self-deprecating, Jamie had his own take on the role of Antoinette's occasional boy-bangle. 'I pretty much ride in on a horse, shag her, go to a couple of parties, have some breakfast, and ride out,' he told a magazine.

There was no doubt that Jamie's sculpted abs had most likely won him the part but quite sensibly he wasn't going to complain, as the role would mean getting on the first rung of the acting ladder.

His girlfriend Keira, meanwhile, shared little of his relaxed attitude to the job and, experiencing something of a role reversal, she was reportedly slightly concerned at Jamie's lengthy and intimate rehearsal time with stunning Kirsten. 'His character Hans is a courtier and admirer of Marie Antoinette and his love goes unrequited. Keira has made it pretty clear to Jamie that once the cameras stop, he's all hers! They do have to get pretty up close and personal to be fair,' a film source revealed.

Meanwhile, getting up close and personal with his real-life lover was proving to be difficult and cracks in his relationship with Keira were starting to appear. They undoubtedly loved each other but there was a hefty list of factors working against them. A trip to Glastonbury Festival was a case in point. Keira had splashed out £3,000 on a Winnebago (type of large luxury camper van) at the Somerset site for what was supposed to be a cosy love-in, with the occasional band thrown in for good measure. The couple had hoped for a romantic weekend with friends at the legendary music event, which boasted a secluded VIP area to hide in if Keira's presence in the muddy compound proved too much. The two-day saga seemed to start off well … Keira was caught snogging Jamie in the hospitality area by journalists but seemed remarkably carefree about her exploits, telling a newspaper, 'I'm loving every minute of the festival. The rain and clouds appear to be following me – we had massive thunderstorms while filming *Pirates Of The Caribbean*. Jamie and I are staying in a Winnebago – you wouldn't catch me in a tent!'

However, as the press caught wind of the fact Keira and Jamie were mingling with the public in a rare display of openness, the fun, festival atmosphere started to lose its charm for the couple. Photographers were hounding them and snaps began to emerge of the pair walking hand in hand, their heads bowed and faces contorted with stress as they tried to make it across the muddy festival arena without getting in harm's way. The media interest had become so intrusive that Jamie no longer wanted to leave their camper van. It was depressingly clear that leading a normal life with Keira as his girlfriend was now out of the question.

Remembering that period of time, Keira told *Vogue* magazine in 2012, 'I literally had no life outside of acting, and I just wanted to go off and not be "on" all the time, not be photographed. I once went to the Glastonbury Music Festival and was completely surrounded by packs of paparazzi the entire time, so I ended up sitting in a trailer, unable to go out.'

When they eventually ventured out to a VIP bash for a friend's birthday away from the prying eyes of the press, two drunken partygoers launched themselves onto the pair, determined to make their lives miserable by shining torches in their eyes and mocking Keira's accent. 'It was an invitation-only event but somehow these two drunk Danish guys managed to get in. Everyone had been having a great night until they arrived and Keira and Jamie were acting more lovey-dovey than ever,' a partygoer remembered. 'For some reason they picked on Keira and seemed hell-bent on getting a reaction. They were taking the p*** out of her voice and being extremely loud and annoying.

'Keira smiled and tolerated them at first, but when they talked so loudly over her conversation, she started looking daggers at them. After the torch shining incident and the rude way they were teasing her about her posh voice it all got too much.'

Keira and Jamie left the party to go to a nearby bar but the two men followed and, in a menacing move, sat at a table opposite them. 'She could probably sense a confrontation brewing so she grabbed Jamie and left,' a friend recalled. 'She made the best of the rest of the weekend – but this definitely put a dampener on things.'

As soon as they returned to London, Jamie and Keira were seen recovering at London's swanky eatery Nobu, where they indulged in comfort food and some much-needed romantic time out. 'They were holding hands over the table in a discreet section. But there was no mistaking the look of love. They were laughing so much it was heart-warming,' an onlooker told a newspaper.

However, behind the scenes, all was not well. Jamie was shaken by the experience and his hatred of the press had already taken root. Keira also openly admitted that she wasn't the easiest person to live with, as she worried incessantly about the cinema releases of her two latest films, *Domino* and *Pride and Prejudice*. 'I'm naturally pessimistic. I don't get carried away with things. I can be a moody cow,' she revealed.

Acting had at that point devoured her life and several years later she admitted that the time when she was dating Jamie was incredibly stressful. 'I wish I hadn't been [such a hard worker]. Life would have been so much easier,' Keira told *Harper's Magazine*. 'I was spending so much time being neurotic and beating myself up that I thought actually, if I didn't, I might get further by just going, "Oh, f**k it".'

Instead, it was her relationship that took the hit.

Jamie and Keira finally split in August 2005. Traditionalist Jamie could no longer cope with her fame and they had started to argue about the fact that he was struggling to accept Keira being the breadwinner. 'There is a big pressure when you go out with someone like Keira. You can feel a bit second-rate and that's what started to happen. It's not like I was bringing the bread to the table – and that can start to affect everything,' he said. 'The man is meant to be the Alpha in the relationship on the money and power front and clearly I was not. You feel you have to be dominant in other areas and that leads to problems. If the person with you in a relationship has more power in terms of occupation, they don't want to think, "Oh, he must find it really awkward because I make loads of money".'

Jamie and Keira were having crisis talks on an almost daily basis and they finally decided to part ways. Friends were adamant that his career in acting also played a role in their split. 'When Jamie announced he wanted to broaden his repertoire and try acting as well as modelling Keira was really supportive. While the idea of them both sharing the same profession was romantic, the reality is they were starting to see less and less of each other,' a friend explained. 'When she comes back from a shoot she shuns showbiz parties and enjoys a quiet life with people she loves around her. But with Jamie trying to crack the big time he's not often around. That's very hard for a young couple to withstand.'

As newspapers scrambled for stories, Jamie's agent also released a statement confirming the break-up. 'Keira and Jamie had decided to call a halt to their relationship in its current phase but they remain completely committed to each other as friends and will continue to see each other in this capacity,' it read.

It was true to say that both Jamie and Keira were still young and, with the next natural stage for them being marriage or children, it was also a case of wrong place, wrong time. 'We all need romance in our lives but marriage and living happily ever after is not something I think about at the moment and certainly won't for a while,' she told a newspaper a week after their split.

Clearly heartbroken, she also went on to describe handsome Jamie as her ideal man: 'I'd go for someone who is a little bit brooding and somebody you can have a good conversation with, a good fight with, who will always keep you guessing and make you laugh. And he has to have good shoes.' But Jamie was gone. She had asked him to move out of her Maida Vale flat and, having handed back the keys, he was now living in a nearby apartment close to Notting Hill with his sister Jessica.

While he was enjoying spending some time out of the spotlight, with evenings in and home-cooked meals, Keira was drowning her sorrows with friends. After she was spotted looking the worse for wear on a night out in London, a friend said, 'She's been on the town with the girls for a couple of boozy nights out. And although she's still distraught, it's done her the world of good.'

'I'm lucky in that I have a great group of mates and I can do my talking to them,' she told *Now* magazine at the time. However, hot on the heels of the story of her split with Jamie came the 'news' that Keira had fallen in love with a new man: Kaz James, the frontman of band Bodyrockers.

The actress had met the handsome Australian at a *Vanity Fair* party earlier in the year and had allegedly been spotted enjoying a string of dinner dates with him since finishing with Jamie. 'Keira really likes Kaz, they are really into each other. She doesn't want to rush into a full blown romance though,' a source said at the time.

A month later, rumours of a love triangle were sparked when Jamie and Kaz came within minutes of a face-off at the premiere party for Keira's *Pride and Prejudice* film. 'It was like a scene from a Jane Austen novel,' one newspaper mused. 'She sent Kaz to her suite at The Dorchester hotel to wait until the wee hours for her arrival. A clever move because just moments after she gave Kaz his marching orders, Jamie arrive at the bash.'

However, the rumours appeared to be just that. Keira claimed that she had never met Kaz, while he admitted some months later, 'We never dated. People said, "Oh poor Kaz", but she never had the chance to break my heart.'

Keira, who in the meantime was still filming the two *Pirates of the Caribbean* sequels, was astonished to hear of the stories back home about this alleged new man in her life. 'I only know about him because I've become rather obsessed with it and I keep looking on the internet. But I never met him. Never! Apparently he's dumped me now. It's the easiest break-up I've ever been through!' she said.

Keira was, however, struggling to cope without Jamie in her life and both of them were devastated about the break-up. Vowing to be friends, it wasn't long before they met up, and the chemistry between them was hard to dismiss. On a day out in the West End together, the couple enjoyed a heart-to-heart while strolling through a park, before doing some shopping. They also stopped to peer into an estate agent's window to look for a new apartment, before cuddling in a taxi on the way back to her flat.

Although friends dismissed their so-called two-month reunion as nothing more than sex, Keira admitted that it wasn't as easy as just saying 'goodbye' to Jamie. 'Things change slowly and it isn't simply a matter of moving on,' Keira commented days after their split. 'A relationship, as everyone knows, is complicated.

'It's not black and white – it's various shades of grey. So there's no way to explain what happened in a paragraph. There's no way you can explain a relationship. To anyone reading this I'd say "Try it". You're looking at a whole set of complex issues.'

A friend of the couple had another take on their brief reconciliation: 'Jamie knows Keira's a free agent. To be honest, she just rings him up whenever she fancies a bit of exercise.' However, it was clearly a bit more than that. A month after being spotted out together in the capital, Jamie admitted that they were back together and this time he was determined to make it work. 'He can't bear to think that he let one of the most beautiful women in the world slip through his fingers,' a friend confided.

'No matter how long you've been with someone, you're wary of letting your guard down. You don't want to say you love them or admit you're wrong. Things are never as straightforward as they seem,' Jamie himself said. 'Let's just say that I hope things work out.'

Sadly, they didn't. By the New Year, it was quite clear that things weren't right and Keira ended it once and for all. 'The person who finally said, "Okay, that's it, I've had enough" was Keira,' he revealed, insisting that it was a lot more complicated than just being 'dumped'. 'But I think it was a culmination of factors and of course we're both so young. It has been my only long-term relationship. The word "marriage" scares me but who doesn't think of that kind of thing after a certain amount of time? But I'm too young.'

It was an inevitable conclusion to all those who knew the couple personally. Always ambitious, Keira had badgered her parents to find her an agent when she was just six years old and made her first TV appearance at eight. By the time she was sixteen, she'd already starred in Brit film *Bend It Like Beckham* and was commanding £3 million a movie. Her rise was meteoric

– unlike Jamie's who was infinitely more modest in comparison. 'Sometimes I don't know whether it was really Keira or me who ended that relationship,' he said. 'It was the culmination of many factors. Because of all the media attention and everything that goes with it, it was not always an easy relationship. We've both got a lot going on.'

His palpable sense of loss – a grief – also started to revive feelings that he'd experienced after his mother's death when he was just sixteen. As well as Keira exiting his life, he would also be saying goodbye to her mum Sharman, someone who had been a big part of his life over the past two years and had become a confidante and good friend.

In an incredible admission – and one which showed the true extent of his feelings for Keira – Jamie said that he had found it harder losing his lover than facing his mother's death to cancer. For the young model, the devastation of splitting from his girlfriend, knowing she would go on and find happiness elsewhere, was impossible to cope with. 'Losing Keira is a very different kind of grief,' he said. 'The strength I got from losing my mum isn't helping me deal with it. When you feel that you've lost someone, it's very hard.

'To be honest, I am not as strong in love as I am in the face of death. Obviously losing my mum was a horrible thing and it's still horrible to this day. But I knew a lot more horrible stuff would happen and it has, to be honest.'

Jamie was hurting. He'd never experienced true love like he'd felt for Keira, nor had he experienced such gut-wrenching heartache when they split. While Keira spoke of regret, Jamie seemed sad and vulnerable. 'I'm coping fine,' he said at the time, 'but I do feel very hurt at times. Things could be worse, couldn't they?'

He had been under no illusion that his beautiful girlfriend's filming schedule took precedence over playing happy families but he was now left with the deep frustration of being referred to as 'Keira Knightley's ex-boyfriend'.

As he had done in the years following his mother's death, it was time to take stock and strike out to succeed in his latest quest: to become an actor in his own right and secure a record deal. His band was poised to sign a recording contract with Sony and, in a statement to the press, his agent revealed what the now world-famous clothes horse had up his sleeve: 'Jamie is an actor but he's also a musician. His primary focus is his music.' When it was suggested that the male model had until now been best known as Keira's boyfriend, his spokesman replied caustically, 'Well, I would dispute that.'

If there was one positive thing to be taken from his heart-shattering split, it was that Jamie had a renewed determination to prove the world wrong – he was not just a six-pack bit of arm candy. 'I know I must protect myself,' the ambitious model told a newspaper a few months later. 'Don't worry my barriers are up – I'm ready for battle!'

Chapter Six

GOING SOLO

'Our sex scenes were a lot of fun, my chest was naked but I kept my pantaloons on below! Kirsten had to perform in bed wearing slippers while holding a fan which was bizarre,' a single-and-loving-it Jamie gushed. 'She's gorgeous. We had no problems with our sex scenes.'

His first foray into acting opposite Hollywood beauty Kirsten Dunst, playing her courtier lover in *Marie Antoinette*, couldn't have gone any better. She was beautiful, the on-screen chemistry between them was electric and the male model was overjoyed that this relatively modest role in a costume caper seemed like a giant step into the movie industry. Moreover, the production was impressive and sumptuous. The crew were given unprecedented access to Paris's impressive Palace de Versailles and some scenes were shot in Vienna; the wardrobe was created by Italian costume designer Milena Canonero and the shoes were made by fashionistas' favourite, Manolo Blahnik. Even luxury French bakery Ladurée was drafted in to make pastries for the film – including their trademark multi-coloured macaroons.

Jamie was justly impressed. 'I was watching the filming on the monitors and next to me was one of the best directors in the world, I had to pinch myself!

'The director Sofia Coppola had everything under control and I think she made a great job of the film,' he told *The Sun* newspaper.

The whole experience had given him a flavour of what a future on the silver screen could hold and he was desperate for more. Although his agent immediately vowed to find him new acting projects, it was decided that, in the meantime, Jamie should plough all his energy into music.

Single and with the media still referring to him as being 'the man Keira dumped' or 'Keira's ex', Jamie was ever more determined to get the girl out of his mind and secure a record deal. 'It's quite frustrating actually, I was doing what I was doing long before I met Keira. I'm in the studio the whole time at the moment.

'I believe something good will always happen if you don't try too hard, if you plan things you just get disappointed.'

Meanwhile, Jamie's reputation for being a playboy bachelor had started to gather pace and his association with Keira was starting to fade. Those in his inner circle hoped that the dating rumours which seemed to be following him, as one of the best looking men in the fashion industry, would also help with a little self-promotion for the model-turned-pop star – and ultimately sell records.

His admission of fancying his co-star Kirsten during their raunchy sex scenes hit the press, as did stories that he had been on a string of dates with actress Sienna Miller. 'Jamie is going to be a teenage pin-up when Marie Antoinette comes out,' one journalist swooned. 'His looks are totally dreamy and since Keira dumped him he's the guy everyone wants to be seen with. Sienna is no exception, they've been out to dinner and she's in love.'

Jamie, who had by then turned twenty-three, struck up a friendship with stunning Sienna after they became neighbours in London's Notting Hill, soon after he parted ways with Keira. He had moved into the apartment that he shared with his father Jim; this was an arrangement that suited them both, since his dad was regularly flying over from Northern Ireland to visit hospitals in the capital.

Sienna, meanwhile, had recently moved out of her boyfriend Jude Law's nearby house, after splitting in a blaze of publicity caused by the revelation that he slept with his children's nanny. They were both in need of some cheering up and, with a host of mutual pals, they quickly became friends with plenty in common. 'They meet up regularly at the Electric private members' bar,' a friend divulged. 'They both sit there supping pints together and have a bit of a laugh. They both need it.'

However, Sienna wasn't the only one purported to be bedding handsome Jamie. Also hitting the headlines was a rumoured fling with Hollywood actress Lindsay Lohan. Jamie was now well aware of his playboy reputation and, although clearly amused by the attention, was quick to dismiss the claims: 'I know the girls I've been linked with but that's all there is to it. If you're seen out together, people automatically think you're a couple. Of course that's not the case. I'd be a very lucky guy if they were all true!' Keen to prove that he was happy with his single status but would be ready to move on if the 'right one' came along, he added, 'I make the best spaghetti in the world. If I was trying to impress a girl I'd probably whip up some pasta and serve it with a nice bottle of red. But there's no one special at the moment.'

'Off-screen I'm not usually very good at seduction,' Jamie admitted in another interview to *The Sun* newspaper about his role in *Marie Antoinette*. 'I'm shy but I had to become Axel in the film so I used a few cheeky smiles which hands up I've used off camera too. But there's no Mrs for now.'

Truth be told, Jamie was ploughing all his energy into music, focusing on securing a record deal with his childhood band, an 'Irish folk duo' called Sons Of Jim. After his first split with Keira, Jamie started to heavily promote one of the band's tracks – 'Fairytale', which was available for download – and during one interview, he admitted that he was still in love with his ex. 'Sure I like my loved ones to hear my music and if that's Keira then alright,' he said.

Music industry insiders then claimed that the band's profile was about to ramp up a notch, with Sony Records interested in signing the pair. Record bigwigs were said to be watching in the wings to see how their singles sold through their band website before making their move and handing them a deal. Jamie and his former schoolmate David Alexander felt confident that they had enough experience: they had performed on/off for five years and recorded tracks together for eight. It was therefore just a case of trying to prove to those that mattered that they could turn their passion into a career.

It was the ideal time to do it – Jamie was dabbling in modelling and had enough time on his hands, while David had been studying law at Newcastle University but was desperate for a future in music. Now was the time to start presenting themselves more formally as a band, so they started to tour Irish and London bars and clubs. Jamie also wasn't shy in boosting publicity for the band and was happy to explain how 'Sons of Jim' came about, describing, as mentioned previously, that the band name was in honour of their fathers. 'Dad's an amazing guy,' Jamie told *The Sun* newspaper. 'My mum died from cancer of the pancreas when I was sixteen. She'd been ill for about a year and a half – afterwards Dad helped me pull through the grief. He's the strongest person I've ever met.

'It's lovely that I can respect him through the name of the band.'

Everything about their music so far had been independent of a label. They had posted their singles on their MySpace band page, where they interacted daily with fans on a busy message board. Although in the early days Jamie and David had 'mucked around' recording tracks back in Ireland, everything had changed in late 2004 when they caught the attention of legendary music producer Brian Higgins. Famous for producing songs for Girls Aloud and the Sugababes, Higgins thought the boys had real potential and invited them both to his studio in Kent where he ran his famous Xenomania production house.

The studio was legendary. Higgins had set it up to establish 'a

Motown-type set-up' with the artists, writers, musicians and the entire recording business all under one roof. Venturing inside the inspirational creative hub gave Jamie just the impetus he needed to finally take his music seriously. It was exciting, intriguing and, best of all, he was about to work with some of the biggest names in music. No-nonsense Higgins was notoriously picky about who he would work with and in an interview with *The Observer*, surrounded by gold discs, in the same month he started working with Jamie he said, 'If you're a production house, you're supposed to work with anyone and everyone: that's the rule, but if we don't feel excited by the prospect of the artist, then the record's going to be shit [...] if we'd made records for everyone we'd been asked to over the last couple of years, I'd be a husk of a person by now. There'd be loads of money around, but the music would be terrible, and the depression would be raging through me.' Jamie was clearly one of the lucky ones and admitted at the time, 'For the last three months I've been working with a really big producer in London called Brian Higgins and we've been recording.

'That's what I've always wanted to do, even before modelling, and, luckily, modelling opened the door for that to be more accessible.'

Higgins immediately set the boys to work and collaborations followed with some world-famous writers and producers – for example Tim Kellett, whose then twenty-year music career included playing keyboards for Simply Red and working with a string of artists such as The Lighthouse Family and James Morrison.

In early 2005 Sons of Jim joined KT Tunstall on her UK tour in a bid to warm them up for a future inside the industry. Jamie and David began to feel that there was a conceivable chance they could finally get signed to a label, and the experience was incredible. The six sell-out gigs, including dates in York and Liverpool, cemented their aspirations to try to make it big, as they got first-hand experience of what life on the road was like for the Scottish recording artist, whose single 'Suddenly I See' had hit the Top 20. 'Touring with Katie was brilliant fun; she's quite incredible. We did six dates with her, so not a huge tour together,' Jamie remembered. 'Watching her do what she does every night was a real treat, and she was completely lovely as well.'

Hailed as 'one of the success stories of 2005', KT's debut album *Eye To The Telescope* had gone multi-platinum and stayed in the Top 10 UK album chart for an impressive two months. In the meantime, Sons of Jim's profile was slowly improving as they made their debut TV appearance on Irish channel UTV's *The Kelly Show*, where they performed the track 'Fairytale'. The pair's husky vocals, with Jamie on guitar, drew rapturous applause from the studio audience. In an all-too-common move, the TV host declared, as he introduced the band, that Jamie had split from Keira just 'a few months ago'. It was clear the model-turned-musician was still coming to terms with the split and having it so publicly rubbed in his face must have made the pain all the worse.

In fact the misery he felt during that period of his life was starting to show in his songs and when Jamie sat down to write new single 'My Burning Sun' in December 2005 with songwriter Ali Thomson, the feelings were still raw. Fed up with dark, gloomy winter days and 'smothering feelings' of isolation, they wanted to write an uplifting track. '"My Burning Sun" acknowledges the way a particular person can reach you and transform your outlook, making life brighter,' music magazine *Billboard* described the music. In the track, Jamie wrote, 'I'm sitting here watching nothing I start to drift away/Thinking about the future, though my clouds are grey/A cigarette and some chocolate don't ever pacify/There's gotta be some daylight through the darkest sky/You could make it alive.'

Although the single wasn't released for another year, it still managed to slip under the radar for the obvious links it could have drawn to Keira, with the lyrics clearly reflecting his residual feelings for his famous ex.

Despite this oversight, it still managed to create a stir when it was made available for download from the band website in 2006, having been released on their own label Doorstep, aptly named after their favourite sandwich shop back home in Belfast. Jamie, clearly excited about the band's potential success, explained how they had got lucky in a newspaper interview, 'Management caught wind of the demo we'd made and so Dave finished his law degree and for the past year we've been concentrating on it.

'While he was doing his finals we supported KT Tunstall. Things started to take off a bit and now we've released a single.'

On the back of it, the folk duo were starting to perform at a number of prominent acoustic venues across London and reviews were beginning to come in thick and fast. 'While the pair admire the post-punk and ska influences of English bands such as the Kooks, they have eschewed this achingly hip path,' one critic raved after hearing the track. 'Instead, Dornan's confident voice anchors a traditional-rock sound reminiscent of Counting Crows. Their lyrics, meanwhile, are more romantic and fey than say the spikiness of the Arctic Monkeys.'

However, it was at a showcase in May 2006 that one of Jamie's songs, 'Only On The Outside', was picked out by critics for looking like it was describing his relationship breakdown to Keira. It therefore became clear to Jamie that no matter how hard he tried to distance himself, it was going to be near on impossible to shrug off the interest and intrusion that his ex-girlfriend generated.

The run-up to the show at London's Teatro club had indeed been tough for Jamie, as Keira had found new love in the preceding few months with her *Pride and Prejudice* co-star Rupert Friend. While she – the glittering film star who was set to earn £50 million within the next two years – was appearing arm in arm with handsome Friend at the Oscars, Jamie had been performing to a modest crowd in an upstairs room in London's private members club The Cobden. It was yet another reminder of the discrepancy in their status.

In this latest track, 'Only On The Outside', Jamie sang, 'I can see your fancy friends trying to steal your innocence/you're so weak around them.' He reportedly told *The Mirror* afterwards, 'The song hurts so much when I sing it. It's about the difficult times in a relationship. We were so in love.' Prominent articles in the press followed, claiming that Dornan's 'song for Keira' was about his 'heartbreak' for the pretty star.

Exasperated, he decided to publicly dismiss the stories as false. Jamie was not one for speaking officially to newspapers, choosing instead to keep his life as private as possible, but this time he wanted to set the record straight. 'Considering Dave and I write together, I can't work out how it could be true,' he said. 'People read into the lyrics what they want, I have no control over that I'm afraid. It wasn't difficult to sing because it was about Keira. I just meant that because it's so high I found it difficult to reach the notes!'

Jamie and David were at that point laying down tracks in the studio for a debut album under the guidance of Cliff Jones, the frontman of the 1990s pop act Gay Dad. Keira was still on Jamie's radar in that they met occasionally as friends, but dinners out with her were few and far between because of the actress's busy schedule and her inability to meet in public places due to unwanted press attention.

The rawness of their split was also starting to fade and far from being emotionally ruined by their parting, as the press continued to claim, Jamie was no longer pining for Keira. His single status was more the result of being 'useless' with women rather than despair for his lost love. 'Ever since I split with her there have been reports that I'm heartbroken. Do I look heartbroken? Of course I'm not. I'm single now and very happy. But that's not to say there's no time for romance!'

Although Jamie wasn't dating anyone officially, he continued to flirt with the world of celebrity and the handsome model

A fresh-faced Jamie Dornan attends the *King Arthur* film premiere in New York in 2004.

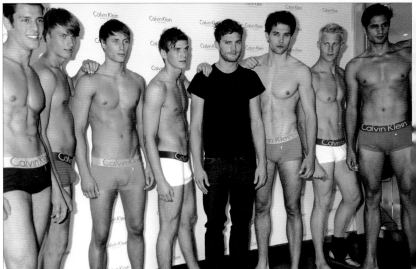

Above left: Jamie at the DKNY Night Fragrance launch in London 2007.

© *Nick Harvey/WireImage*

Above right: Signing posters at the '9 Countries, 9 Men, 1 Winner' Calvin Klein photocall on Oxford Street in 2009.   © *Dave M. Benett/Getty Images*

Below: The news in briefs: Jamie poses with fellow Calvin Klein models.

© *Dave M. Benett/Getty Images*

Above left: At the afterparty of the European premiere of *King Arthur* with girlfriend Keira Knightley in London's Guildhall in 2004. © *Dave Hogan/Getty Images*

Above right: The gorgeous couple attend Glastonbury Festival in 2005.

© *REX/Anna Barclay*

Below left: With co-star Rose Byrne at the premiere of *Marie Antoinette* at the 44th Annual New York Film Festival in 2006. © *REX/Carolyn Contino/BEI*

Below right: Fooling around with Sienna Miller at an event at Tom's Kitchen in London, 2007. © *REX/Richard Young*

Jamie and his beautiful wife, Amelia Warner, attend a post-BRIT party at the Savoy Hotel in London in 2013.

© Dave M. Benett/Getty Images

With his acting career taking off and celebrity friends, Jamie Dornan becomes one to watch.

Above: With Sony's Amy Pascal, Kirsten Dunst, Sofia Coppola and Sony's Sir Howard Stringer at the *Marie Antoinette* premiere in New York.

© *E. Charbonneau/WireImage*

Below: Amelia and Jamie attend a preview of 'Second Floor', a photographic exhibition by Sam Taylor-Johnson in 2014.   © *REX/Richard Young*

Sharing a joke at Alfred Dunhill Links Pro-Am Championship Gold in
Carnoustie, Scotland in October 2014.   © REX/Ian McIlgorm

Above: On the red carpet with Amelia at the BAFTA TV Awards in London in May 2014.
© WILL OLIVER/AFP/Getty Images

Below left: Posing with his award for Actor in a Lead Role in Television at the Irish Film and Television Awards in Dublin in April 2014. © *Phillip Massey/WireImage*

Below right: With *Fifty Shades* author E. L. James at the GQ Men of the Year Awards at the Royal Opera House in September 2014. Jamie clutches his Vertu Breakthrough award.
© *David M. Benett/WireImage*

Model-turned-actor and international heartthrob, Jamie's star is well and truly on the rise.

flew to Cannes in May 2006 to publicise *Marie Antoinette* with the rest of the cast and crew. Amongst the champagne parties and soirées aboard million-pound yachts, there was also the all-important debut screening of the film at the French film festival.

Despite his overwhelmingly positive experience on set, to his dismay the movie got booed during its showing to an audience of critics, writers and film-goers who didn't like Hollywood's treatment of the life of the Austrian-born queen. At a press conference afterwards, Coppola – who had previously directed box office smash *Lost In Translation* – admitted that she too was 'disappointed'. 'It's better to get a reaction, it's better than a mediocre response. Hopefully some people will enjoy it. I think it's not for everybody,' she added.

Insiders hoped that its much younger target audience would make the movie a success in the long run and Jamie was determined to see the positives in the disappointing situation. Whether the historical comedy-drama was going to be a flop or not, it had at least got the model noticed … and that was something Jamie was actually getting rather good at.

Along with making strides in his music career, Jamie had recently landed a massive contract as the face of Dior Homme. The offer was incredible: for three days' work in Buenos Aires, he was paid – up front – for a three-year exclusivity deal. Although he wasn't exactly propelled into Keira's financial stratosphere, this made him an extremely wealthy young man. 'They pay you well upfront, so it looks like you're working a lot harder than you are,' he admitted.

Jamie knew he was onto a good thing and while he had

somehow landed a semblance of an acting career with no formal training whatsoever, some of the world's top designers were also scrabbling to hire him, which was no mean feat, as competition for such major contracts was fierce.

The casting with Dior designer Hedi Slimane at the helm had resembled elements of the reality TV show *Model Behaviour* for which Jamie had auditioned five years previously, with hopefuls getting eliminated in stages until the judges are left with just two finalists. Although Jamie had failed to make the final cut in the TV version, in the real world he came away with first prize.

His brooding good looks had secured him the enviable contract as the face of the fashion house's much-hyped fragrance campaign for Dior Homme and once again, he was perplexed that he'd been handed such a prestigious role. 'Why am I the face of Dior Homme?' he said in an interview at the time. 'At Dior, they kept eliminating people until it was down to two. I wasn't really focused on it at the time, you know. I don't really know why Hedi chose me. I'm not the best-looking guy around.'

Reflecting Jamie's nonchalant attitude to the casting, the photos featured the striking model posing effortlessly alongside the aftershave, in a crisp white shirt and black jacket. It was a print campaign with snaps appearing in glossy magazines, newspapers, billboards and bus stops … Jamie's face was starting to pop up everywhere, all over the world. 'It was effective casting, and it got people's attention,' David Farber, style director at *Men's Vogue* magazine, said. 'Clearly he wasn't the typical model. He read rather like a "real" person but he obviously wasn't some skinny waify model boy they found on the street.' Another admirer drooled, 'He has the square-jawed profile of a Roman senator.'

The six-figure contract also meant that he reportedly had enough cash to buy into the two-bedroom home he shared with his father in Notting Hill – and Keira was replaced with another new love: a 1988 silver convertible Mercedes-Benz called Maisie.

Jamie was well aware that his success was due to the fact that he photographed like a dream, and he was quite clearly happy to run with it until something else cropped up. It required little effort and, despite being baffled as to how, he was quickly travelling down the path towards becoming the highest-paid male model in the world. Landing a fragrance campaign like Dior Homme is the holy grail for models, with adverts running for months at a time as do the residuals, meaning that Jamie was now earning serious money. 'It's a great business for now, a great way to make money and have a laugh. Who knows what's next?' he said shortly after the Dior campaign. 'I put a lot of what's happened so far to luck and right place, right time.'

Although he hated the hours of sitting around in his underwear getting bored, he loved meeting the outlandish creative types inside the fashion industry; also, it was a business so lucrative for him that it would have been mad to have given it up to go to drama school as he'd originally intended.

Despite the healthy cash flow and stunning good looks, Jamie knew he wasn't perfect and one of his massive and unmistakable flaws was being a complete disaster on the runway. Even though he could pose and preen for hours in a studio, Jamie was still useless on a catwalk. Dior was one of the first fashion houses to discover his bouncy gait and, in order to avoid embarrassment for all concerned, quickly amended his contract so that he didn't have to appear on the catwalk when opening their shows. 'I got everything out of the world that you can get. And I never did a fashion show,' he said proudly. 'It was part of my Dior contract to open its show in Milan [...] but we had that written out as I have a funny, bouncy walk – not cool. It wouldn't make a suit look any better.'

While his modelling career was ticking over nicely, his so-called 'acting career' was in fact proving to be something of a flash in the pan. Firstly, *Marie Antoinette* was not as successful as everyone had hoped. The initial reviews were mixed. American film critic Roger Ebert gave the film four stars out of four, whereas website *Rotten Tomatoes* scored it 55 per cent in positive reviews, describing it as: 'Lavish imagery and a daring soundtrack set this film apart from most period dramas; in fact, style completely takes precedence over plot and character development in Coppola's vision of the doomed queen.'

However, *People* magazine's movie critic, Leah Rozen, was quick to pan the film and wrote in her wrap-up of the 2006 Cannes Film Festival: 'The absence of political context upset most critics of *Marie Antoinette*, director Sofia Coppola's featherweight follow-up to *Lost in Translation*.

'Her historical biopic plays like a pop video, with Kirsten Dunst as the doomed eighteenth-century French queen acting like a teenage flibbertigibbet intent on being the leader of the cool kids' club.'

The film grossed $15 million in Northern America and $61

million worldwide, making it one of the few underperformers for distributor Columbia that year. In the UK, the movie took only $1,727,858 in box-office sales. It wasn't the best news for Jamie but, undeterred by the film's flop, his agent had lined him up for numerous auditions – all of which, to Jamie's embarrassment, failed. 'I mean f***ing hundreds of auditions,' he said. 'Some of them totally humiliating experiences. People attach too much to the idea of being a model that you can only be a certain way to have done it. You will always be dealing with it.

'You're an actor who used to be a model, who never trained; there are not many directors queuing up.'

For the time being, though, he had aspirations of being a rock star which helped to keep him positive. 'It's fun being able to play your music and people listening to it and responding well. You get a real buzz. I think there is part of me that does want to lift off and go a bit more Chris Martin, jumping around the place.'

The night before his homecoming gig in Belfast's Auntie Annie's club, Jamie admitted he was set on concentrating on one thing at a time. 'When I'm doing my music, I put my all into it and when I'm doing my modelling or acting, I do the same. At the moment I'm really busy with the band so I put everything into it.

'I see them all as different things. They're three different jobs, I work really hard on all of them and I can make it all work, I believe, to a credible extent, if I'm willing to put the work in.

'Someone told me they thought I would land on my feet and I probably believed them too much. But from that point I stopped worrying about everything.'

As it turned out, though, Jamie had plenty to worry about – and this time it wasn't Keira. It was his beloved dad. Behind the scenes, his whole world had turned upside down again.

Chapter Seven

THE BIG 'C'
STRIKES AGAIN

Jamie's father had cancer. It was a devastating blow to the Dornan family and it hit his three children hard. He certainly didn't seem particularly ill but the truth was that he was very sick indeed. To all those who knew him it seemed impossible. How could such a strong and energetic man – at just fifty-seven years of age – be struck down with the same disease that had taken Jamie's mother just seven years before?

Professor Dornan had been a real guiding strength throughout his children's difficult childhood years, and it was both cruel and inconceivable that someone so crucial and present in their lives now faced his own mortality. After all, he was Northern Ireland's most successful obstetrician, drove a sports car, was happily remarried, went to the gym twice a week and played golf. 'Professor Jim Dornan, the colourful Obstetrician Gynaecologist, with an insatiable zest for life,' one journalist wrote by way of introducing the famous doctor in an interview on his incredible forty-year career in medicine, during which he delivered 6,000 babies.

Ever since the death of his first wife Lorna to pancreatic cancer when Jamie was just sixteen, there was no doubt the Dornans, as a family, made a point of seizing the moment. Despite his troubled teenage years, Jamie had somehow found the strength to push ahead with life, determined to grab whatever good opportunities came his way – a positive attitude which was undeniably due to the example set by his father.

However, life had changed again and abruptly at a time when Jamie was at his most vulnerable. His father broke the news just as Jamie was coming to terms with a life without Keira. 'My dad is one of Northern Ireland's top obstetricians. He's been ill with leukaemia for a while,' Jamie admitted in 2006 in the wake of becoming single again. 'Despite all the treatment he still isn't in remission. Dad's an amazing guy. My mum Lorna died from cancer of the pancreas when I was only sixteen. She had been ill for about a year-and-a-half. Afterwards Dad helped me pull through the grief. He is the strongest person I've ever met.'

Rather unusually, Professor Dornan had discovered the cancer himself. He made the self-diagnosis while staying at the luxury flat in London that he co-owned with Jamie, while on a business trip to the capital. The busy doctor regularly jetted over from his home in Belfast to meet with colleagues at the Royal College of Midwives, and the Royal College of Obstetricians and Gynaecologists, where he was vice-president at the time. It was on a short walk home from the Marylebone institute one evening when he realised just how 'utterly and totally' exhausted he had become.

When he got indoors, and with Jamie out for the night with friends, Jim had some rare time to himself and he started a train of thought, which was to bring devastating results. 'I did think anything could happen to anybody. It did come as a very great shock though to some of my friends that I did actually make the diagnosis myself.

'I was in London at the time, at the Royal College, Jamie and I owned a flat and he was out one night and I was just so tired walking up past the college, I was just knackered.'

In reality, he had known that something hadn't been right for some time; first of all, just looking at himself in the mirror he could see that the man in the reflection was clearly anaemic. The signs for anaemia – meaning someone has low iron levels in their blood – include a pale complexion and breathlessness or tiredness due to low oxygen levels.

All the key symptoms were there; however, nothing in his lifestyle had warranted them being there. He ate very well – Jim himself admitted he was a dab hand in the kitchen, just like his son Jamie – exercised moderately and wasn't bleeding. Nevertheless, the father-of-three was also overwhelmingly tired; thus far he had put it down to being overworked and stressed. He was approaching retirement age, after all, and had a jam-packed life both in and outside of work, which was showing no sign of slowing down. 'Just before my own diagnosis was made I was simply completely exhausted. Using the good ol' never failing, retrospectroscope, I had taken on a lot while giving up nothing. Pressure and stress. How often do you hear those words?' he explained.

As he finally took time to stop and think about it, though, he realised that being both anaemic and so fatigued were also key signs of cancer. He became certain that he had some variety of leukaemia; his symptoms pointed to the probability that a problem in his bone marrow had triggered the anaemia, since he could rule out the more common and less serious causes for the blood disorder.

He vowed to go for a blood test as soon as he returned to Belfast the following day. The journey back to Northern Ireland and the twenty-four hours that followed, during which he underwent a string of medical tests, were without a doubt harrowing for Jamie's father. Worse still, the results confirmed exactly what he had suspected. 'For twenty-four hours I knew it and then I got the confirmation,' he said.

Hearing those words for the first time when sitting on the other side of the doctor's table was deeply frightening for the father-of-three. 'The words Cancer and Leukaemia weren't new to me when I heard them directed to me personally for the first time, but I do admit that when they come right to your front door you soon realise you can't run out the back one,' Professor Dornan said almost a decade later. 'I was terribly fearful.'

Having delivered babies for over thirty years, Jim was used to experiencing extreme emotions – from the wonders of seeing a healthy child come into the world to the devastation of delivering a stillborn – but nothing prepared him for the moment he was told he had cancer and stared his own mortality in the face.

He had also seen his much-loved first wife and cherished father die from the cruel disease, and now it was his turn to sit in the patient's chair. He knew more than anyone how this could all turn out – as did Jamie – and the thought of losing both parents to the disease was without a doubt terrifying. 'My day-to-day work as an obstetrician brought me daily highs and lows associated with the total pleasure and joy associated with a successful outcome, and the often total sense of loss associated with a tragic outcome to birth.

'But rarely did I have to actually deal with cancer professionally. When I was thirty-four my wonderful dad died of cancer at the age of sixty-two. And when I was fifty, my similarly aged fantastic wife died the same way,' he said.

Professor Dornan, as is the case for any other patient, had to follow the usual protocol for getting the right diagnosis, with blood tests and a bone marrow biopsy to determine the exact nature of the disease. Initial tests proved that it was indeed leukaemia, a cancer of the cells in the bone marrow. These white blood cells deep in the bone – known as blasts or leukaemia cells – are not formed normally and multiply. As well as feeling tired and getting anaemia, symptoms include bleeding and bruising problems, and having an increased risk of infection.

His self-diagnosis had been spot-on and Jim found himself joining the 2,750 people diagnosed with the disease in the UK each year. As if that wasn't enough to take in, he was told that it looked like an aggressive form of the cancer, meaning that it could be potentially impossible to treat. Jamie's father began to prepare himself for the fact that he may die within a matter of months. 'I went into the hospital thinking I may never come out again […],' Jim said. 'Initially they over-diagnosed it and thought I had a more serious type of leukaemia than I had.'

However by the following day, and thanks to further explorations, it was discovered that the cancer could at least be controlled – even if it was incurable. 'It was Chronic Lymphocytic Leukaemia (CLL),' he said. 'It made sense now. After all I ate well and was not losing red cells […] simple as that. After a few early hiccups the diagnosis was confirmed.'

CLL is different to other leukaemias in that it tends to develop very slowly and patients can have it for months or years without showing many symptoms. 'Within twenty-four hours the doctor came in and said, "Hey, it's not the leukaemia we thought you had, we've done some tests and it's called CLL," which can kill people but can run along very quietly at the bottom of the barrel.' It was indeed a better prognosis than they had previously thought but Jamie, along with his sisters, was told the terrible news that there was no cure.

To make matters worse, Jamie's step-grandfather – Samina's father – was also diagnosed with leukaemia at the same time. Unlike Jim, though, no treatment could curb his disease and he later died. 'Sadly at the time I got my leukaemia, Samina's father got it too but he got a bad one,' he later said. 'Very sadly it killed him … He was a great man, a very honest, a very moral man.'

It was an incredibly stressful time for the whole family but, being a doctor, Jim knew that there would be a good and a bad way to handle the situation. Rather than wallow in fear and self-pity, worrying about the road ahead looking less than easy, he decided that the way forward was to immediately strike up close relationships with the medical staff treating him. 'To cut a longish story short, I got very appropriate treatment and formed a "bromance" with my oncologist! ... As you do!!!'

Consultant haematologist Dr Robert Cuthbert at Belfast City Hospital, who was particularly crucial in getting him the right treatment, was one of the doctors with whom he formed a close bond. The two medical experts, along with a team of cancer specialists, put together his treatment plan and it clearly helped to make the process a lot more bearable. The pair of them started to discuss what therapies were available to him and Jim insisted he wanted to try out medication that wasn't usually prescribed in the Belfast hospital. He was determined to control the cancer and stay in charge of the disease so that he could continue being a doctor, husband and devoted father for many years to come. 'Now it hit me pretty hard and my doctor said "Don't worry I'll just give you these tablets" and they were what we were handing out when I was at medical school and I said "No, you're going to have to come back with something sexier than that,"' Professor Dornan explained some years later. 'So he did go away and make a phone call and came back and said, "Okay, we are going to do that, that and that."'

Blood transfusions followed, as well as some intense antibody-based cancer treatments. Although the Republic of Ireland had been issuing leukaemia patients with the revolutionary therapy for some years, the NHS at the time – in 2005 – wasn't prescribing the life-saving therapy because it hadn't yet been approved by the regulator, The National

Institute for Health and Care Excellence (NICE). Frustrated that it wasn't offered as a matter of course, Jim insisted on trying it anyway to pave the way for future CLL patients. 'It's really frustrating that only last year did NICE come back and say yes that's the treatment people with this kind of leukaemia should be having,' he commented. 'Yet at that time I was the first person in Northern Ireland to have it. I wasn't a guinea pig, in the Republic of Ireland everybody had been getting it, but the way the British Health Service works is that one: "Does NICE approve it" and two: "Can we afford it?" before it actually goes out there, so I have a problem with NICE actually because I don't think they should make those decisions.'

Much to his son Jamie's relief, Jim immediately started the new treatment using 'monocle antibodies'. The clever therapy uses man-made versions of immune system proteins, or antibodies, which attach to the cancer cells and kill them. The medication, given by injection, is effectively a second immune system designed specifically to attack the leukaemia. As the weeks turned into months, slowly but surely the lifelong treatment was keeping Professor Dornan's cancer under control and at bay.

Jamie's father was in remission but ultimately the cancer could return. At last he was getting the right treatment but the world-famous doctor admits he was terrified in the wake of getting diagnosed with cancer, mainly because the medics treating him in Belfast didn't believe he had many years left to live. 'During one of my early treatment cycles I asked one of the young buck oncologists "Do you think I'll see 80?"

'In truth I expected him to say "Oh now, none of us know

how long we have, and there are new developments every day. Why, I remember a man …"

'Instead of which he just looked at me, and then looked at the floor and said nought. As his head went down, my heart went down.'

Hard as it may have been, the Dornan family had to get back to work, trying to function as normally as possible in tough circumstances. Jamie continued visiting his dad at the luxurious home in Cultra, County Down, which he shared with his devoted wife of four years Samina. Nothing was put on hold: Jamie's stepmother carried on overseeing a revamp of the family home in between her career in medicine and their busy social life, while Professor Dornan, remarkably, still remained focused on his work. Delivering babies every week was a reminder indeed of the wonders of life, and being immersed in such a rewarding and life-affirming environment helped him to forget his own troubles.

Behind closed doors, however, he now admits that he was very frightened of dying and faced an uncertain future until his job took him to the Arab state of Oman, where he was examining postgraduate doctors some months later. Thankfully, he finally found a medic who put him at ease. 'I met a fantastic Iraqi haematological oncologist who had been driven out of Birmingham by racist neighbours. He was, and is, a gentleman. I was sitting having a coffee with him and the subject of my cancer came up.

'I was hugely buoyed by his positivity. So much so that I felt strong enough to ask him the same question,' Jim explained.

Unlike the young doctor back in Belfast, this medic believed that, thanks to the wonders of modern medicine, there was every chance that he could live for decades. 'His answer? "I don't know whether you'll make eighty or not, but I doubt if it'll be CLL that'll kill you." What a great answer,' he remembered. 'Of course I had, and indeed have, no right to live to eighty, but I do have the right to hope to live to eighty.'

With renewed positivity, Professor Dornan returned home to Belfast determined not to let his cancer blight his life and that of his wife and children. As the months turned into years, it turned out that the Iraqi doctor had been right all along, and Jim found that he could continue leading a normal life, with the leukaemia under control.

Sunday roast dinners with the family – a favourite with the Dornans – rounds of golf at the weekend and much-loved holidays in South Africa with a group of old friends were all back on the cards again. This spectacular country had long been a favourite with the doctor after his work had taken him to hospitals and conferences in Cape Town; it had become a place he liked to return year-on-year with pals for a cathartic trip away.

His zest for life was indeed infectious and Jamie – sharing his dad's hope for the future while remaining stoically philosophical – plunged headlong into his music career. 'My dad was diagnosed a year ago. It's just one of those things. He's alive and away in South Africa on a boys' trip. He's in remission. I kind of think if all this happens before I'm twenty-three then the road ahead will be quite smooth.'

Luckily for the young and ambitious Jamie, the following years would indeed be filled with fun and fortune, and his father would still be there shouting him along from the sidelines.

His father, meanwhile, admitted that there was no stopping him, as he gave up his job in the NHS to go into private practice despite heading towards retirement age. 'I have a very fertile mind and I always have a few ideas and I like working on them,' he explained in 2013. Speaking about his cancer, he added, 'I'm fine now; I just had a check-up the other day but when you come face-to-face with your own mortality, it is a wake-up call.'

Nine years after discovering his cancer, Professor Dornan was still in 'remission' and at the time of writing, in 2014, Jamie's father was still going strong. 'I'm in remission but I prefer to think of it as "cured",' he said. 'If it returns, we will deal with that when it comes as a second issue. I wish the oncologists would realise that we often think like that.'

Jim was still mindful, though, that his fortune could change at any point. 'I think I'm at peace with myself and also preparing myself that the end could come at any time – I think that's what comes from having a near-death experience. So I'm very aware of that now, so I'm not burning the candle at both ends although some of my friends still think I am,' he said. 'I'm still a driven man and I still want to change the world but I'm also with the realisation the bad news could still come – but maybe it won't come to anything.'

Back in 2005, though, and with his cancer treatment in full swing, it was business as usual for the whole family. 'Jamie's one of the nicest people I know,' his father said proudly just before hearing the news that his model son was on the cusp of getting a record deal that year. 'He is getting on with it and is enjoying himself. I'm incredibly proud.'

With his ever-supportive father's backing, it was now time to conquer those ambitions on his 'to do' list: Jamie had a music career to crack and a modelling career to enjoy, and now more than ever he was determined that nothing would stand in the way of him becoming a world-famous actor. Remarkably, and thanks to the wonders of modern medicine, the most important man in Jamie's life was going to be there every step of the way, rejoicing in his successes and catching him at every fall.

Chapter Eight

THE GOLDEN TORSO

Jamie was now mixing with the rich and very famous as the darling of the modelling industry. The man on everyone's lips was said to be commanding six-figure sums for his contracts and was dubbed 'the male Kate Moss'. Everyone wanted a piece of him.

Jamie was quick to acknowledge at the time that gay men, from photographers such as Carter Smith to designers like Hedi Slimane from Dior, were playing a large role in accelerating his career. He was adjusting well to the heightened interest from males and females, both inside and outside the industry, that such a job brought his way.

Fashion designer Matthew Williamson was one of the many who openly drooled over the handsome model, confiding to a magazine, 'My secret crush is Jamie Dornan, but he knows that – it's not secret.' Whereas some straight men may have felt uncomfortable by the public adoration, Jamie revelled in it. 'I just love the attention,' he told gay magazine *Out* in 2006. 'I don't really mind where it comes from.'

'I find it hard to believe people are actually that interested in me, I suppose it's the Irish charm that gets me the jobs,' he added.

It was fair to say that although most wannabe pop stars would be busking to earn a crust or living on the breadline as they tried to carve out a bona fide music career, lack of money was no issue for Jamie. He was certainly no struggling musician, as he kick-started 2006 with yet another cash injection thanks to new and lucrative modelling contracts with clothing giants H&M and Gap.

With brooding stares now down to a fine art, Jamie appeared in the glossy H&M print campaign dressed in khaki and posing with waif-like blondes on a beach for their spring/summer 2006 collection.

His bank balance was boosted further when Gap snapped him up to join a line-up of faces promoting their 'Age Wash Denim' jeans. It was another opportunity to mix with the fashion elite, as he hung out with prestigious Dutch photography duo Inez van Lamsweerde and Vinoodh Matadin who had been hired by the high street brand to take a collection of slick, arty shots for the Gap campaign. The pair, whose commercial success was linked to their lavish adverts for a string of luxury fashion houses, including Yves Saint Laurent, Givenchy and Jean Paul Gaultier, met Jamie at New York's Pier 59 Studios, along with a team of top stylists.

Jamie was in his element; although he still hadn't warmed to the hours of posing, he revelled in the interesting characters he met on the job. Moreover, Jamie could now call New York his second home and the job wasn't far from his apartment. At just twenty-four years of age, Jamie had his own pad in both the Big Apple and London – the ultimate testament to his jet-setting lifestyle and modelling success.

And it wasn't just the fashion industry that was raving about the young model. Much to Jamie's surprise, the UK press was also maintaining an interest in his personal and professional life despite his broken ties with Keira. 'Find time for a private perv over Jamie Dornan the Belfast-born model in the Dior campaign and the new Gap and H&M ads,' cooed a journalist in a fashion special on Dornan in the *Sunday Times*. 'The brooding beauty used to date Keira but now poor love he's single and heartbroken – cue an X-rated fantasy about how you would cheer up the poor love.'

Not that Jamie needed any cheering up – it was now that he was enjoying one of the biggest contracts of his life: starring alongside Kate Moss in Calvin Klein's new magazine and billboard campaign. He had posed for the fashion house in 2004 and they were back for more of the Irish charmer. Stunning Kate had been handed £500,000 in the deal by the designers who had made her a superstar in 1992. The move to hire her again, however, was deemed massively controversial at the time, since the catwalk beauty was waiting to hear if she would face criminal charges over alleged cocaine abuse. The supermodel had been snapped the previous year snorting a white powder in a recording studio with her then bad-boy singer boyfriend Pete Doherty. The salacious newspaper pictures had prompted a number of high-profile fashion clients, including Burberry, Chanel and H&M, to drop the then thirty-two-year-old from some of their campaigns.

When news came that Calvin Klein had signed up Jamie and Kate as the faces of their new jeans collection, the supermodel and mum-of-one was waiting to see if the Crown Prosecution Service had enough evidence to charge her with drug abuse. However, Calvin Klein campaign creative director Fabien Baron was adamant that they had made the right choice in their casting. 'Kate and Calvin Klein have a long history together and it felt natural to reunite them for this new Jeans campaign,' he said in a statement. As it turned out, Kate wasn't prosecuted due to lack of evidence and her multimillion-pound modelling career was back on track.

The photo shoot itself was incredible and, despite the size of the campaign in terms of coverage and the extraordinary fees handed to both Jamie and Kate, it took just two short days to shoot. Working alongside Kate, Jamie got an enviable insight into what life was like for one of the world's biggest supermodels. In the raunchy black-and-white shots, the good-looking pair posed in a variety of sensual poses, both topless and in dark jeans.

Many had the co-stars down as best pals – and even lovers – after working together, but Jamie was quick to admit that despite appearing together on billboards across the world, they literally spent just a handful of hours in each other's company.

It turned out to be an unforgettable experience for Jamie; as well as starring opposite Kate, he got to work with well-respected fashion photographers Mert Alas and Marcus Piggott. Known as 'Mert and Marcus', the pair were famous for their portraits of sophisticated, powerful women – including Madonna, Jennifer Lopez, Victoria Beckham and Lady Gaga – as well as for their work for magazines and fashion labels. 'The difference between us and other photographers is that we care a lot about appearance,' Alas explained. 'We spend most of the time in the make-up and hairstyling rooms.'

And this high profile ad was no exception. Jamie was seriously pampered and preened for the shoot hosted at Jack Studios in New York. 'As well as the usual hair and face make-up', Jamie said, 'what I do remember about the Calvin Klein ads was a lot of people running me down with dark, oily tanning stuff, I mean, I'm a white Irish guy, it was a problem.'

Once in the studio, Jamie's co-star was charming and the pair got on brilliantly. Barriers had to be broken down immediately, with Kate wrapping her legs round Jamie's waist and pressing her naked torso up against his back for the erotic shots. 'She was really a lovely person – very nice and more shy than you'd expect,' he said. 'But when you're working with someone who is top of their profession it's a real thrill.'

Although Jamie wasn't normally intimidated when working opposite a big name, he couldn't help but feel that she was in a completely different league. Jamie certainly didn't see himself on equal footing with his famous co-star. 'She's an amazing model and an amazing person. Even watching her work is incredible.

I've been mucking around doing this for seven years, she's been doing it for eighteen and she's still top of the game,' Jamie gushed some years later. 'It's a nice compliment but I don't reckon we're on the same playing field,' he commented on his nickname 'the male Kate Moss'.

The campaign was an immediate hit with the fashion house and, once officially launched, it did more than just sell clothes. Jamie was plunged into the centre of religious controversy when it hit America. A huge billboard of the CK advert with a topless Kate grabbing a bare-chested Jamie had been erected outside a mosque. Devout Muslims were reportedly outraged by the image which confronted them every time they went in or out of their place of worship and the press had a field day. 'It's only a matter of time before action is taken. Someone will find a way to cover them up,' one disgusted neighbour told a newspaper. 'Jamie and Kate's CK ad upsets hundreds of muslims,' another headline screamed, while website *animalnewyork.com* sniped, 'We are dying to see what a hastily spray painted burqa looks like on the young coke-sniffing crusader.'

Kate and her boyfriend Pete Doherty had been no strangers to controversy since the start of their relationship twelve months before, and Jamie soon became mixed up in gossip involving the couple, as rumours started to emerge that she had dumped the pop star for the Irish model. Jamie was adamant there was no chemistry between them, pointing out that they'd spent less than a week with each other – and that was at work. They had certainly never 'enjoyed a string of secret dates'. 'I'm not cool enough for Kate,' he told the *Sunday Mirror* newspaper. 'I've met her several times and she's really sweet but I somehow don't think I'm rock star enough.'

Although Jamie dismissed the gossip as ridiculous, his friends didn't think that such a pairing was out of the question and begged him for the inside track on his secret romance. 'My friends ring up asking why I didn't tell them I was going out with Kate Moss?' he said incredulously. 'And I'm like, "I'm not! I worked with her for half a day that's it."

'I honestly don't do love affairs. That's the most embarrassing thing about the whole situation, I never pull.'

While Jamie remained resolutely single, business was good – even though modelling was his bread-and-butter and music was where his heart was. 'It's a great business for now, a great way to make money and have a laugh,' Jamie said soon after the Calvin Klein advert. 'Who knows what's next? I put a lot of what's happened so far to luck and right place, right time.'

However, it was more than just his pretty face that was landing him the contracts; he also had a burgeoning fan base. Jamie's almost naked body was adorning buses, glossy mags and girls' bedroom walls worldwide. Whole websites and pages on the internet were cropping up devoted to the 'Golden Torso', as he was dubbed by the *New York Times* in an article which profiled his up-and-coming *Marie Antoinette* role.

Jamie was also mentioned in a book entitled *Supermodels: 21st Century Lives*, in which he was just one of nine legendary models to be listed alongside Twiggy, Kate Moss, Erin O'Connor and the first-ever male supermodel Marcus Schenkenberg, who reached the peak of his fame in the early 1990s. 'A bit of a pretty boy, Jamie's clean cut and athletic and likes to keep in shape playing rugby. Jamie's not just good looking – he has plenty of Irish charm too,' the book raved.

'I question why all of this has happened to me,' Jamie said at the time, 'I don't see myself as particularly good-looking. I could never have predicted it at all in a million years.' But the public couldn't have been more interested in him and his rippling abs, which even he admitted was rare for a male model. 'You can't take this industry seriously, especially if you are a guy,' he declared. 'This is definitely a girls' industry. It all seems quite strange to me.'

In fact, devoted Dornan followers seemed just as interested in swooning at photos of his body as in learning about the most seemingly boring minutiae of his everyday life. 'My daily routine is a ten-minute shower, a cup of coffee and then I go. I use Aveda Brilliant Shampoo and Dove soap in the shower,' Jamie confided to the *Evening Standard*. As a testament to his down-to-earth nature, he also revealed in the feature that he couldn't leave the house without an iPod and that he kept fit by 'walking a lot. I try to walk everywhere in London and New York and I play Frisbee in the park.'

It must have seemed extraordinary to his friends and family that unassuming Jamie had become such a public fascination. Some of his schoolmates could hardly believe the escalation in his fame and regularly ribbed him by text message or called him on his phone to let him know that they'd spotted him in various sexy poses in magazines, billboards or at their bus stop.

During one interview with a British newspaper, Jamie stopped chatting to the journalist to answer a call from his flatmate who was in stitches after seeing posters of Jamie in his pants for Calvin Klein jeans. It all served to keep the millionaire model grounded. 'He was just laughing,' he explained. 'That's good I need to have that. Some people, they really want all this,' he said of his fame-inducing modelling career.

His family, meanwhile, remained shocked and delighted in equal measure. For Jamie's father, seeing his son's continued success and surprise appearances in the press and on billboards must have come as a welcome distraction from his own problems and cancer diagnosis. 'I think they're proud, at least I hope they're proud. I think they're bemused at my modelling, as am I, that it happened and it's continued to happen for quite a while,' Jamie said of his father and stepmother's reaction to his recent success. 'I think they're happy, none of their friends' sons are doing this so I think it's quite a weird thing for them to talk about. It's a complete dinner party novelty.'

It was also reassuring to see that Jamie hadn't changed a bit. It wasn't so much that he couldn't believe his good fortune anymore – instead, there was secretly a part of him that didn't want to be there. There was an untapped world outside modelling that was his for the taking, if only he could land himself another acting job. That, however, was one area of his life which seemed nothing short of a disaster. Jamie was the first to admit that his good looks and rippling muscles landed him the part in *Marie Antoinette*; his challenge was to get directors to take him seriously as an actor rather than just as something nice to look at.

It was proving extremely difficult. Amongst the castings for modelling assignments, Jamie was being put forward for TV and film roles by his agent, but he rarely got past the first round. 'I literally went to hundreds of auditions. I'd been auditioning for parts for years. I never got any better at it. I'm crap at auditions. I know there are people who can walk into those rooms and make those lines sing on the page and get the job immediately. I wasn't one of them. I'm still not one of them,' he said some years later.

On the back of his role in *Marie Antoinette*, his agent also sent him out to Los Angeles during pilot season – a time between January and April when TV studios cast, produce and test out new shows. Competition is fierce, and the rounds of auditions are relentless and cut-throat, as hundreds of wannabe actors try to get their feet on the first rung of the movie industry ladder. 'It was one of the most dehumanising things anyone could ever go through – on an entertainment level, that is,' Jamie said.

Directors and TV producers in Hollywood were at least polite, which for many made the blow easier; for Jamie, however, this just made him feel even more deflated. The Irishman often walked away from auditions quietly convinced that he'd landed the role until his agent got a call saying that he had once again been unsuccessful. 'There's no such thing as a bad meeting in LA. You walk out thinking that you have the job,' he explained. 'I think I've only ever had silent "nos" out there.'

For the time being, at least, he had plenty to focus on; his busy schedule was packed with music and modelling, and the latter couldn't have been going any better – on paper at least. 'I've never felt massively satisfied from standing there while someone takes my photograph. It's never given me a thrill,' he confided in an interview with the *Evening Standard* magazine years later. 'But it would take a very foolish man to turn down the stuff that was offered to me. You're in your twenties and people are going to give you a silly amount of money to lean against a wall with your head down.

'F**k me, you've got to do it.'

Still down to earth as ever, behind the scenes the model was enjoying an incredibly normal life. 'I still cook spaghetti bolognese and I love a good book.

'My perfect evening in would be with my mate Jake and my sister Jess eating tomato and mozzarella followed by my spaghetti, it's the best in the world! For pudding we'd have cheesecake, drink Pinot Noir and watch South Park on TV,' he said. 'My daily grooming routine is a ten minute shower, a cup of coffee and then I go.

'I always have a book on the go. I couldn't live without books, I don't understand people who don't read.'

Defying the stereotype of a pampered supermodel, Jamie admitted that although he liked to keep fit with morning press-ups, he wasn't into the kind of preening you'd expect. 'I cut my hair myself. I don't have any hair products, I use whatever is to hand.

'I like playing golf but I'm not really into going to the gym, not when I can go for a walk outside.'

His easy-going attitude and undoubted professionalism appeared to be paying off. Select modelling agency, who had handled Jamie's career from the start, was now seeing a steady stream of requests for the young fashion star who could now command £10,000 a day.

Next up was Nicole Farhi's spring ad campaign in early 2007, which saw Jamie star in a series of black-and-white photos in a range of well-cut suits and tailored jackets. Jamie's good luck followed with an advert for Aquascutum, alongside stunning supermodel Gisele Bündchen. The quintessentially English label wanted an image overhaul – from country-set staple to brand of choice for the sexy, modern go-getter – and chose 'uber-suave' Jamie and Gisele to play the smouldering 'power couple' at the centre of their new branding.

Key pieces in the collection included clothes based on original designs worn by Audrey Hepburn, Sophia Lauren and Lauren Bacall in luxurious fabrics. The shoot was at sprawling country mansion Cliveden House in Berkshire – made famous in the 1960s for the Profumo affair – with legendary photographer Mario Sorrenti at the helm. Best known for his spreads of nude models in the pages of upmarket magazines *Vogue* and *Harper's Bazaar*, the steaminess of this project was no exception, and Jamie was quickly directed into producing a set of sultry shots with the Brazilian beauty. 'Jamie is a real pro, he can produce "sexy" in a second,' a fashion industry insider said. 'For the camera he oozes seduction effortlessly and at the same time makes female models feel at ease; he's friendly, polite and a joy to be around. He's one of the best male models around.'

The campaign was a massive success thanks to the undeniable on-camera chemistry between Jamie and Gisele. 'We are thrilled by this new campaign,' said Aquascutum president and CEO, Kim

Winser. 'Gisele and Jamie are the perfect pairing to communicate our creative vision for the new season.' As the photos of the handsome pair in well-cut, luxurious outfits draped around each other and oozing sex appeal hit the internet, fans online gushed, 'They are so hot! Yay! I love them!' Another wrote, 'Stylish, sexy, classy and eye-catching, Jamie looks stunning!', while a fashion journalist commented, 'These two look like they're made for each other. Jamie Dornan is exquisite.'

Hot on its heels was Jamie's new contract as the face of Bvlgari eyewear. Posing in a series of black-and-white shots wearing the famous designer glasses, Jamie again attracted reams of online attention from both men and women. 'He's so hot,' one male fan drooled on a fashion website. 'I don't normally go for a man in specs but he's changed my mind.'

Unsurprisingly, Aquascutum was back for more of Jamie less than a year later. 'Last season they turned up the heat for fashion label Aquascutum on location at the quintessentially British Cliveden House and this season, Gisele Bündchen and Jamie Dornan are back to do the same for the brand,' an article in *Vogue* proclaimed in July 2008. This time the pair's photocall was to pose against the scenic backdrop of London's St Paul's Cathedral – and the photos wouldn't look out of place in the new *Fifty Shades of Grey* movie.

'In one shot, the woman – dressed in clinging black dress and spike-heeled Manolos – lies seductively across the man's lap,' a journalist said of the campaign in Britain's *Daily Telegraph* newspaper. 'Elsewhere, she is captured in executive-style sharp tailoring in an office overlooking St Paul's, while he is pictured straddling an MV Agusta F4 – the "Ferrari of motorcycles"– in a chic trench.

'Nom doms? Bankers immune to the credit squeeze? Or a power couple in the clutches of a passionate affair?'

Aquascutum's Kim Winser added at the time, 'I love the passionate electricity; power is such an aphrodisiac.' Jamie was indeed a powerful presence in the studio but while he was pulling in fans with his pouts, he was having little luck pulling in real life. He was desperate for a girlfriend, but he was the first to admit that he was useless in love. 'I really need a girlfriend,' he admitted earnestly in 2007. 'I can appreciate going out and having fun with whoever but there's a real side of me that needs the relationship part.'

Jamie liked the stability that a steady girlfriend afforded and while he loved going out drinking in bars with friends, he enjoyed staying in with wholesome food and a good film on the TV just as much. Few could believe he remained a single bachelor. The press was adamant that Jamie – one of the most desirable men in the world after romancing the formidable Keira Knightley – must have been dating someone.

Within months of splitting from the Hollywood actress, the rumour mill started with stories that Jamie had his eye on other beautiful women. Whenever he starred in a campaign, the model was alleged to be having a dalliance with another new actress or model, even if the details were wildly exaggerated to make the story grittier. There had been Sienna Miller, of whom he admitted thrice-over that she was 'just a good friend' who lived round the corner and shared his love of good food and a gossip. A few weeks later, Jamie had supposedly 'hooked up' with Hollywood actress Lindsay Lohan after the pair were seen huddling together in a quiet corner of a Calvin Klein-sponsored bash in New York to celebrate Kate Moss's new advertising campaign. They were later allegedly seen holding hands, which sparked rumours of a string of dates in the American city.

Dornan later denied even having met her. 'I know who she is, I've seen her movie *Mean Girls* but that's it. There's no Mrs Jamie at all,' he said at the time. Despite his denial, Jamie made it into Lindsay's 'sex list'which she allegedly penned in 2013 on a boozy night out with friends. The actress was said to have scribbled down a list of thirty-six famous men that she had bedded since becoming famous and the countdown of her best-known lovers included Jamie. A source who claimed to have watched her write the document during a booze-fuelled session at the exclusive Beverley Hills Hotel, said, 'It was her personal conquest list. She was trying to impress her friends with the list and then tossed it aside.'

Whether there was any truth in it or not, within weeks of reportedly dating the blonde actress, Jamie was onto another woman. This time, he had struck up a close friendship with *Footballers' Wives* beauty Lucia Giannecchini, after meeting through friends. 'She's trying to keep her blossoming friendship with Dornan top secret,' a source told the *Sunday Mirror* newspaper in an article about the actress's new love interest.

Next up, the rumours that he was romancing Kate Moss surfaced again and due to the ongoing speculation, even years later, that they had been an item, Dornan felt compelled to comment on it whenever he gave an interview. 'I think it's quite hard to meet someone special in London,' he explained. 'There's a whole pool of attractive women in London but I find it intimidating. London is so vast so it makes it hard to know where the nice ones are or what kind of people they are going to be. It was a lot easier when I was at school and you knew everyone you pulled.

'I never dated Kate Moss.'

There was also the added problem that people had started to comment on how well he passed for straight, thus insinuating that he wasn't interested in women at all. 'The amount of people who think I'm gay is astounding,' he added. Nevertheless, girls were certainly flocking to him, even if he didn't quite know how to handle it.

At the V Festival in 2006, glamour girls Alicia Duvall, Caprice and Jodie Marsh allegedly begged the organisers to introduce them to the up-and-coming star, while the then single popstar Lily Allen also made a beeline for him before swapping mobile numbers so that they could meet at a later date. 'Lily rushed over to Jamie who was sitting with a couple of friends. She introduced herself and started nattering away to him,' an onlooker said of the chart-topping daughter of comic Keith Allen. 'He seemed taken aback at first but soon they were getting on like a house on fire. They had a couple of beers together and then got out their mobiles and typed in each other's numbers.'

Even if a long-term romance wasn't on the cards, he was certainly enjoying some one-night flings and his playboy reputation was now at full throttle. The Calvin Klein hunk was spotted kissing Australian model Gemma Ward in the Louis Vuitton VIP room at London's trendy Movida Club a few months later, before chatting up her supermodel pal Lily Donaldson. Meals out with stunning brunette model Lily Aldridge also followed. Even though he wasn't actually dating her – she is supermodel Saffron Aldridge's half-sister and her best friend is singer Taylor Swift – it was quite clear Jamie was now circulating with the cream of London's society girls.

He was also hot property with Hollywood A-listers, and *O.C.* star Mischa Barton made her feelings known to Jamie after being introduced by mutual friends at the Cartier Polo International in Windsor. Jamie and the pretty blonde enjoyed a day together at the exclusive sporting event before going onto the after-party at London's plush China White nightclub where they spent the night 'giggling and laughing' in a quiet corner of the exclusive bar.

Talk of an ongoing romance was nothing more than speculation but Jamie was soon out wining and dining another beautiful woman – this time supermodel Lily Cole. Jamie and the stunning redhead indeed made a beautiful couple and they both clearly enjoyed each other's company; they lived within ten minutes of each other in West London and had a shared passion for eating hamburgers, despite their enviable slim physiques. The duo had gone together to an Armani fashion show in the capital, where Lily, who had taken a break from her social and political science degree at Cambridge University, was also modelling. Both had a string of mutual friends inside the fashion industry and it was clear that the press loved the idea of the celebrity pairing. 'She is quite taken with Jamie. They were having dinner at Locanda Locatelli near Oxford Street recently and couldn't take their eyes off each other,' a source told the *Mail on Sunday* newspaper. 'Backstage at Armani Lily wouldn't let him out of her sight.' One of Jamie's admirers wrote on a fan page, 'It's an unusual pairing but they're both brainy so maybe it works,' while another observed, 'He's too shy and worried about rejection to go out with anyone. Lily and him know each other through work.'

Jamie was adamant that there was no one special in his life. Friends of the model, meanwhile, claimed that amidst his evenings out with friends and potential lovers, his sister Jessica had tried but failed to reunite him with Keira. She had remained in touch with the actress, since they had plenty in common to justify being friends. 'Keira and Jessica got on well when she was dating Jamie and the two women remained chums,' a source told the *Daily Express* newspaper. 'With Jessica's help, Keira has met up with Jamie as a friend and has even been to see him in his new home. Jessica would do anything for Jamie from cooking for him to propping him up emotionally.'

It was true that Jamie hurt after losing Keira, but he didn't want to go back; it had been too hard for the model to cope with being the underdog in their relationship. Although they met up for a few meals here and there over the course of the next year, they simply drifted out of each other's lives for good. 'We're great friends and we do meet up but I'm not heartbroken, do I look it?' he said at the time. 'I don't think so. I'm just getting on with things, as is she.'

Keira was indeed making great strides without Jamie and rumours of marriage to her new partner, actor Rupert Friend, were starting to do the rounds. 'It's all very well for Keira Knightley who's been prattling on about her plans to buy a London house with her boyfriend Rupert Friend,' columnist Adam Helliker wrote in the *Sunday Express*, 'but spare a thought for lovelorn model Jamie Dornan who has not found a girlfriend since the actress flung him out of her bed. Quite why handsome Mr Dornan, 25, should have subsequently experienced so little success in his boudoir form is something of a mystery.'

While others seemed mystified by it, Jamie didn't really care about his single status, since professionally he was on a roll. Perhaps the best part of his current occupation was that modelling shoots that lasted only a day or two, funded him for months and left him free to do what he actually wanted to do: music. 'If I am doing a film I might have to take time out from being in the recording studio as I might be away on set. But when it comes to modelling it isn't like you're away on month-long assignments – it doesn't take that long to take a photo,' he explained. 'You're only away for two or three days here and there and a lot of the time you're in London anyway. I find it easy to balance things – and I still have a lot of spare time to do nothing.'

Not that he had time to do 'nothing'; Jamie was very busy indeed.

Chapter Nine

JACK OF ALL TRADES

'This boy is a veritable model slash everything,' proclaimed *Out* magazine in 2006. Indeed, Jamie had his fingers in many pies. Not only was he trying to make it into the Top 40 with Sons of Jim, he was still playing rugby, which he hadn't stopped doing since being picked up by the Belfast Harlequins in his teens. He also swam regularly, played golf, indulged in yoga and religiously started every day with fifty press-ups.

His dogged determination in everything he did was astonishing. The music career soon after his split from Keira appeared to be bang on track. Sons of Jim had found management in Los Angeles and a dream partnership with music producer Brian Higgins, as well as a UK tour supporting KT Tunstall under their belt.

Jamie and David's two singles – 'Fairytale' in 2005 and 'My Burning Sun' a year later – released on their own label Doorstep had sold an encouraging number of copies through the internet alone. The pair had publicised the band themselves, and even produced a professional-looking album cover for 'Fairytale', with the songwriting duo posing on a bridge with leather jackets and matching grey scarves.

Sales for the EPs were encouraging and running into the hundreds; they performed regularly in a string of top London nightclubs, including Carling Academy in Islington, as well as appearing in more unusual venues like the Vans shoe store in the capital's popular Carnaby Street. Jamie was determined to crack the music industry in whichever way was necessary and it wasn't so much the venue that mattered, but rather the audience they would be reaching out to.

Charity appearances were also on the cards and the duo joined sporting heroes, boxing champ Barry McGuigan and Northern Ireland football manager Lawrie Sanchez, in the summer of 2006 for the BBC's Sport Relief Mile in Belfast. After running the course, Sons of Jim performed to a crowd of adoring fans in Belfast's Custom House Square.

Jamie was no stranger to many Belfast locals and found an immediate rapport with the audience. This was probably helped in no small part by the fact that his modelling career was followed scrupulously by the local newspaper, the *Belfast Telegraph*, and he was well-known to the city's rugby fans as he had been playing for the Belfast Harlequins from the age of fifteen.

Indeed, as a teenager and young man in his twenties, rugby remained one of Jamie's real passions, and he wasn't prepared to give up his childhood aspiration of being a successful sportsman anytime soon. Amongst the modelling campaigns, he was still managing to find time to play – and not just back in Belfast or London but also in matches across Europe. Jamie continued to play his favourite position of winger for a local team until he was twenty-four, as his wiry frame and fast pace meant that he was ideal for the job. 'I've played on the wing since I was about eight. I've always needed to bulk up so until the modelling took off I was ramming Big Macs down my throat and doing plenty of bodyweight work. I'm over the Big Macs now, but I'll still drop down and do press-ups whenever I find the time,' he said of his lifelong passion for the game.

After a match in Sweden, three years after his split from Keira, Jamie thought that his rugby-playing days might be numbered after badly damaging his knee. He said of the tournament, 'I was doing okay, but when I turned to run past one of their backs I found I no longer had that extra speed I once relied upon. Instead I go swimming as often as possible.'

Normally placid and easy-going, watching rugby was also one thing that could make Jamie's blood boil. He clearly cared a lot about what happened on the field and was furious if Ireland lost. 'The last time I lost it was watching Ireland play rugby,' he admitted. 'I got very angry because we lost – I was heartbroken. I get bad road rage as well, a lot of swearing!'

In between the weekends away getting sweaty on the rugby pitch, Jamie ensured that he also made time for his friends and family. It was important for him that amongst the glitz and glamour of modelling he remained grounded, knowing all too well from experience that fame can quite easily disassociate people from their loved ones. As he had no real friends from the modelling world 'because you only spend a few hours with models at a time' it was his school friends from Methodist College in Belfast that meant the most to him. They had always been the glue that kept him together during the darkest of days and he was under no illusion: the good times could end at any moment.

He was also constantly reminded that life was extraordinarily precious by his father's updates on his ongoing cancer treatment. While Professor Dornan 'had more energy than any man I know', it was undeniably hard for Jamie to cope with the thought that his only surviving parent had the same disease that killed the other – even if his father, unlike his mother, was able to fight it. Despite father and son often being hundreds of miles apart from each other – with Jamie either being in London or New York and Jim's job taking him away from Belfast to hospitals across the globe – they tried to meet up as often as possible.

Jamie, who wasn't keen on emailing and social media sites on the internet, insisted on a more traditional way of keeping in touch by sending handwritten letters to his dad. They also shared a passion for roast dinners on a Sunday and would try to enjoy a leisurely, lavish meal whenever they came together.

Jamie also kept his friends close at hand and nights out with the lads in London or back in Belfast were important to the now famous model and singer. One of Jamie's greatest loves was a night out with his mates before curling up in bed with a good book. Despite his newfound career which traded off his handsome physique, he still didn't believe he was anything special. 'I never had any reason to think I looked any different,' he told *Vogue* magazine some years later when asked about his good looks while he was growing up.

True to his word, and clearly not precious about preserving himself for the camera, Jamie became legendary for opening bottles of beer with his teeth and enjoyed necking back pints of Guinness like his life depended on it. 'I absolutely love the stuff,' he said, 'although I've overdone it a little recently thanks to four weddings back home in Northern Ireland,' he said at the time. 'I guess I'm just lucky with my genes,' he replied when quizzed about how his body looked unaffected by his alcohol consumption.

Like most men in their twenties, he found that drinking was a sociable way of relaxing and forgetting about work – although Jamie could be known for overdoing it. 'I've woken up on my stairs, curled up like a cat, one or two times after big nights out,' he told *The Sun* newspaper when asked if he'd ever woken up somewhere strange. 'I also woke up on the plane from Vancouver on the way here, just as they announced we were landing in London. I'd had a few drinks before the flight and don't remember getting on the plane, so waking up was a bit of a shock!'

However, one night the high jinx took a turn for the worse when Jamie found himself embroiled in a terrifying fight. Drunk on his favourite beer, the model was out drinking in Infernos bar in Clapham, south London, when he told a fellow drinker that he was being rude, which was particularly uncalled for since it was

'National Courtesy Day' – a fact he had learnt from watching UK daytime TV show *Today With Des & Mel* that morning. Furious with the comment, the man headbutted Jamie, leaving him with a broken nose. Instead of going to hospital, he staggered home, swallowed some ibuprofen, slept fourteen hours and awoke covered in congealed blood. 'It's not a story one would associate with the ambassador for the Calvin Klein lifestyle,' a journalist wrote afterwards.

To be fair, the incident was quite out of keeping for Jamie, who is known by his friends as 'Daddy Dornan' for being one of the more sensible and self-controlled within his group of friends. 'When I go out with my mates, we're a big group of Belfast boys and at the end of the night we can get a little, you know, hyperactive.

'But I tend to get my sensible head on and can be quite strict with them, like "Calm down lads". Which is why they call me Daddy Dornan.'

It was just as well that Jamie's natural instinct was to stay in control, since fans were starting to come out of the woodwork on his precious nights out. While he'd been propositioned before over the internet, Jamie began to find that he was being approached by fans, as his fame meant that he was becoming instantly recognisable. Women had started to come up to him and chat him up, which took Jamie completely out of his comfort zone. A meal out with friends in London one night took a difficult turn for the model when an older woman approached him and wouldn't leave him alone. 'There was lots of me going "Oh really?" and turning away and mouthing at my friends for help and lots of her pulling at my shoulder and asking, "Would you like some of my drink?" No way, I don't know what you've put in it!' he explained.

Jamie found the interest bizarre and although it was nowhere near the level that he had witnessed with his ex-girlfriend Keira, being approached by strangers left him feeling uncomfortable. Jamie's feelings were compounded further when a man came up to him on the street and begged him to sign a poster showing the model wearing only pants. The fan explained that he was his 'inspiration'. 'I found that weird, signing my own crotch, thinking "Don't be inspired by a man who happens to look all right semi-clothed". There are so many things you could be inspired by. I mean it's OK to be inspired by a woman in pants! Oh dear […] not that I'm suggesting that women's only purpose is to look good in pants.

'I just think men being idolised because they look good in pants, that's a bit ridiculous isn't it?' he added.

While modelling left him cold, ever since his split from Keira he had ploughed all his drive and ambition into making a success out of his band, Sons of Jim. Music had always been important to him and he was obsessed with it. 'My iPod would never get stolen at the gym. No one else would listen to the stuff I work out to […] Roy Harper, Led Zeppelin and The Kissaway Trail they all help me escape and channel my energies into my workout.'

He was also star-struck by fellow musicians and, despite experiencing his own fame, was intimidated by bands that he deemed talented and had made the big time. 'I once saw Wayne

Coyne, lead singer of The Flaming Lips in a New York coffee shop. I didn't even meet him and I was completely star-struck. He's an alarmingly cool guy,' he explained.

Jamie and his co-star David weren't short of fans themselves. The press were hailing them as 'Dylan-esque' and a 'modern day Simon and Garfunkel', which both admitted was 'a very great compliment'.

On the release of their single 'Fairytale', a soft-rock ballad which he described as 'an edge of homegrown rock', people had started to sit up and listen. The striking duo had also won fans while on the road with KT Tunstall, and Sons of Jim had sold a decent amount of singles online.

However, there was an element of self-doubt when it came to his music; the model was out of his comfort zone. 'It's a bit nerve wracking being in this business but we're not expecting to rule the world or anything, we're not Coldplay. We're putting some music out there and if people like it then great and if they buy it because it's good music then that's all we want,' he said at the time. Jamie was convinced that he would never make it big and definitely wasn't expecting to make any real money out of it. 'There are so many artists out there who I respect an awful lot who don't sell millions of records but one thing's for sure – their fans do respect them and love the music.' It was something he really cared about, though, unlike his ever-increasing modelling assignments. In stark contrast, Jamie could pull these off with such ease that he had stunned even the world's top photographers and, consequently, they earned him mega-bucks.

It was quite obvious that Jamie was looking for recognition

rather than reams of cash and while admitting that his first acting role opposite Kirsten Dunst was 'very cool', that particular avenue had dried up for the time being, so it was only sensible to concentrate on making a success out of the band.

The reality is that deep down Jamie knew that it wasn't his strongest talent. In fact, in years to come, he would claim his music was 'terrible'. 'I did have a band. A terrible band called Sons of Jim,' he admitted in 2012. 'I sang and played the guitar and a whiney harmonica. I would have enjoyed the band more if we'd been good. You need to believe you're the best band in the world for it to work – even if you're not. I just didn't believe in what we did.'

Reviews of the band had also become mixed and some critics had panned the duo. 'It's not that they're a bad band it's just that their sound is nothing new,' one wrote. 'I'm sorry, I don't know what the fuss is about,' said another online review. 'It would have been far more interesting if he'd come clean and admitted the single was about Keira, then I would have bothered listening to the track all the way through.'

While the music double act had enjoyed the benefit of working with music producer Brian Higgins, who had helped a number of high profile pop acts, it was quite clear that they weren't happy with their change in sound. Jamie felt that they were moving at right angles from where they wanted to be musically. 'It was one of those things that moved on its own wave that we weren't really surfing on,' Jamie explained to *Elle* magazine. 'I was young and with one of my best mates in the world – who still is one of my best mates in the world – and we were just having fun, but other people were trying to make us go in a direction we hadn't envisioned. Eventually something has to give.'

It wasn't long before Jamie and David had to sit up and realise that the record label wasn't going to sign them, nor was their management going to get them gigs in venues any larger than local clubs or student unions. 'We were crap,' Jamie admitted. 'The management tried to go, "Hey, a model and whatever," and make it a pop thing. We were pushed into something a bit rotten actually.'

It was obvious that their music had taken a turn they weren't happy with and certainly wasn't getting the kind of recognition they'd hoped for. Sadly, the closest they got to a Top 40 hit was their single 'I Heard' topping the charts in Brunei, covered by local star Hill Zaini. Jamie also had unexpected and amusing success in Malaysia some years after Sons of Jim had disbanded. 'I was on YouTube and I clicked on a link and it was this Malaysian guy with Faye Dunaway and Kristin Kreuk from the TV show *Smallville* in a video for a song that I wrote,' he explained. 'It was number one in Malaysia, so I'm waiting for the cash.'

Apart from there being little chance of them making any real strides in the music industry, while Jamie was able to support himself through extremely profitable one- or two-day modelling jobs, David – who had studied law at university – had his own day job to pursue. It just wasn't going to work.

Anyone could see that Jamie was now at a crossroads in his life and had clearly suffered from the curse of the 'all-rounder'. He excelled in so many areas that it was difficult to know which interest he should really be following for the best. 'I knew I wanted to act and was always trying to find my way into it. But there were always distractions. I was still involved in modelling contracts, still mucking around being in a band. It's that thing you do if you're trying to do something creative and you're young and you haven't pinned it down yet. You try to do lots of things and see what floats your boat,' he said.

It had taken almost a decade since leaving school to have the opportunity to really follow his heart into acting but finally his next acting break was just round the corner. There had been rumours for over a year that Jamie was set to crack it. Initially, there had been the story that Jamie was to present a cookery show for Irish broadcaster UTV. He was supposedly one of a line-up of celebrities, including former Miss World Rosanna Davidson and chef Gary Rhodes, to present *The Fabulous Food Adventure*, a new daytime series. Then there were stories that he was to star in 2007 Bollywood movie *Namastey London*. Apparently, the director Vipul Amrutlal Shah was considering either Jamie or Sean Connery's son, Jason Connery, to play the second lead in the Indian blockbuster film based in the UK capital.

While the role never materialised, Jamie finally struck it lucky with his first lead part in a movie. Straight-to-internet film *Beyond the Rave* was to be the first Hammer horror movie since 1979 and was going to be directed by Matthias Hoene, who later became famous for his comedy horror *Cockneys vs Zombies*, starring Michelle Ryan, Richard Briers and Honor Blackman.

By lucky coincidence, it was at his sister's wedding that he met the movie's producer who started chatting to him about the project and asked if he'd like to be involved. After necking 'plenty of booze', Jamie agreed and the deal was sealed. After all, he needed all the acting experience he could get. 'I met the producer at my sister's wedding and was very fond of him. I liked what he was trying to do with the project, and after plenty of drink, I said I'd be involved. Then I was involved and it was a mad shoot,' he admitted some years later.

While it was hardly the most conventional way of landing a role, *Beyond the Rave* had all the hallmarks of being an interesting and well-publicised project, which would have appealed to Jamie, as he wanted to gain as much exposure as possible.

The famous film company Hammer Film Productions, known for its gothic 'horror' movies from the mid-1950s to the 1970s – including Dracula and Frankenstein – was revived in 2007 by a Dutch tycoon and the movie was to be its first since *The Lady Vanishes* some twenty-nine years previously.

Simon Oakes, who took over as CEO of Hammer and confirmed that the sum of £20 million was going to be ploughed back into the studio to make new films, said, 'Hammer is a great British brand – we intend to take it back into production and develop its global potential. The brand is still alive but no one has invested in it for a long time.'

Jamie, in the lead role of Ed, was 'honoured' to be at the centre of the studio's revival and it was an interesting role to say the least. Jamie was to play an English soldier who had to find and win back his girlfriend from the clutches of bloody thirsty vampires, disguised as a group of hard-core ravers, before he flew back to Iraq in the morning. It was a four-night shoot for very little pay but Jamie was more than willing to put his all into it. 'The whole shoot was a night shoot. I was sleeping all day, having no life, and then getting up, going to work at six in the evening and coming home at six in the morning – very strange.

'I don't remember a great deal about that time. But I made good friends. We were brought together through the lack of sleep,' he told *Interview* magazine. 'It was 5 per cent of the budget of a television series, pulled together with string and chewing gum. Jamie wanted to get more into acting. He was committed on set, doing a lot of his own stunts. We spent four nights working together – all-night shoots – and he really got his hands dirty,' director Matthias remembered some years later.

Although working on the film had been great fun, it never became a cinema release and was instead shown exclusively on internet website MySpace; the experience, however, had proved invaluable for Jamie. Moreover, he was in good company, with a strong cast which included Sebastian Knapp – playing head of the vampires Melech – who had a string of TV credits such as the BBC's *Silent Witness* and ITV1's police soap *The Bill*. Irish actress Nora-Jane Noone, famous for the 2002 movie *The Magdalene Sisters*, meanwhile, played opposite Jamie as his girlfriend Jen. 'The credits are huge for what is an outstanding production and good luck in the future to all those who played even small parts,' film critic Jaci Stephen wrote in *The Guardian* newspaper. 'Much of the brilliance lies in some laugh-aloud lines […] For some, it's a happy ending; others lose their lives fighting tooth and nail for survival. I won't give it away, but let's just say that after his last night of leave, if Ed survives, Iraq will be a breeze!'

Jamie twice now had had the taste of working on a movie

and absolutely loved it. He was in no doubt that being a film star was his destiny and jokingly admitted that he felt primed to appear opposite Hollywood beauty Angelina Jolie in a romantic comedy – although he wasn't sure that he could outdo British actors Colin Firth and Hugh Grant who were legendary in playing those kinds of roles. 'I'd love to do a romantic comedy with Angelina; she's kind of flawless to me,' he said. 'Sometimes I think it's harder to be a leading man in a romantic comedy if you're not English. I think the English do that really well that sort of slightly camp, pathetic thing. I'm not sure Angelina would want to do a romantic comedy with me though. I'm not saying Colin Firth or Hugh Grant are pathetic, far from it! I think they are both great but I would like to have a crack at it.'

Although Jamie was grateful to have had the opportunity to star in the movie, he was the first to admit the genre of film didn't appeal to him at all. 'I'm not a horror fan at all. It's just not really my scene,' he said. Hard-hearted horror devotees weren't fans of the movie either and as soon as it hit the web, film bible IMDb. com was flooded with negative reviews. 'I managed to get a look at this and it was cheap, cheap, cheap, a low rent, throwaway cash-in on the Horror name,' one viewer wrote.

'It's really depressing that the Hammer name is being associated with him and that a new generation of filmgoers will associate this with the once great horror studio.'

Although within a week the IMDb.com critical rating had shot up to nine-point seven out of a possible ten points – which led to one critic quipping, 'Jamie Dornan shouldn't let his mum loose on the internet' – it later slunk back to a five out of ten.

Jamie was now on the lookout for larger roles and although his comments on now looking to act opposite Angelina Jolie in a blockbuster were taken as a joke, there was truth in what he said. He was dreaming big.

It was, however, back to the drawing board for the time being – at least back to the modelling studio where Jamie continued to carve out a top-notch career. Jamie continued to be the face of Dior, and his Aquascutum adverts with Gisele Bündchen were seemingly everywhere, which led to an ever-increasing number of fashionistas and teenage girls joining the Jamie Dornan fan club.

He had also been welcomed wholeheartedly into London's society scene and could be said to count model Agyness Deyn, Radio One DJ Nick Grimshaw, Daisy Lowe and Sienna Miller among his circle of friends. Of course, he had known many of them from his relationship with Keira, but Jamie was now part of the celebrity in-crowd in his own right. 'Aggy, as she likes to be known, is the Alpha leader of this tribe, which includes It-girl Daisy Lowe and Keira Knightley's ex Jamie Dornan,' the *Daily Mail* reported. 'Their style is a mixture of feminine and masculine; a combination of ballerina and biker all teamed with a strong sense of irony. They all hang out in Pink nightclub in Soho and exclusive private members club Shoreditch House in London's East End.'

Jamie also boasted a number of Hollywood actor pals, including Mischa Barton and film star Josh Hartnett, who dated old friend Sienna Miller in 2007. 'Josh Hartnett is a great friend, but I've learnt not to stand next to him. He's way too tall and handsome,' Jamie said at the time.

The twenty-five-year-old model's name had started cropping up in the society pages of newspapers and magazines, and much to his delight, Jamie was now more commonly referred to as an actor rather than model – or worse still 'Keira Knightley's ex'. 'Spotted! Actors Josh Hartnett and Jamie Dornan sheltering from the rain in the Prince Regent pub Marylebone,' the *Daily Mirror*'s 3AM column printed in late 2008.

A gossip piece in the *Daily Mail* a few weeks later under the headline 'Talk Of The Town' also noted that Jamie had been seen dining in swanky Thai restaurant Diep le Shaker in Dublin alongside a host of famous faces including Rolling Stone Ronnie Wood's ex-wife, Jo Wood. 'Causing more of a stir at table number 12 though,' it read, 'was male model of the moment and actor Jamie Dornan. Jamie the face of Dior is currently single and very much in demand. We spotted owner Alex Farrell hanging out with him at the end of the bar … perhaps he was going to serenade her?'

Ever ambitious Jamie was riding high with his modelling career but his job as a clothes horse, in reality, continued to give him modest satisfaction. The problem was that he knew he could do so much more and he felt he was already acting, albeit under a different guise. 'These images are trying to attain the unattainable,' he explained of him acting out the strong, brooding male on another billboard or magazine page. 'They're trying to take a picture of something that isn't there.'

To the uninitiated, Jamie – the handsome model who could sell a million pants – looked self-confident, brooding, in control and in lust with the gorgeous woman he posed next to on the page. In reality, he was single, terrified of losing his father and desperate to be an actor. He had done incredibly well but true job satisfaction and finding the woman of his dreams seemed, for the time, completely out of his grasp.

Chapter Ten

THE DORNAN FURROW

Jamie the supermodel wasn't ungrateful for his career in fashion; he knew only too well what a fickle industry it was. What made him feel extra fortunate was that his strange walk had been a blessing in disguise, as it meant that he had no chance of being forced to enter the excruciatingly competitive world of the runway model.

Luckier still was his trademark 'look', which was keeping him in business and had become so famous that it even had a name all of its own: the 'Dornan Furrow'. Although new faces dominated the catwalks of Milan and Paris, the world's big brands and fashion houses didn't dare risk putting new people at the front of their campaigns. Dornan was part of the 'old boys club' alongside legendary male models Oriol Elcacho and Steve Gold, who all had a tried-and-tested look that worked and ultimately sold well. 'The resurgence of the supermodel isn't just for the ladies, now more than ever companies are going back to their tried and true favourite male models. Familiar faces like Jamie Dornan are snagging major campaign space,' a fashion magazine in 2009 mused. 'While new faces dominate the catwalks of Milan and Paris the good old boys are front and centre in campaigns. When the stakes are as high as they are now the industry relies on proven talents to push product – nothing beats a face you can trust.'

Giorgio Armani was one of the labels who dared not take a risk and, true to the current trend, snapped up Jamie to front their new campaign alongside Russian supermodel Sasha Pivovarova. The stunning pair were to be the face of their striking spring/summer collection, and Jamie was once again reunited with dynamic photographic duo Mert and Marcus in putting the campaign together. Photo shoots with the highly praised pair were exciting and had the feel of being on a film set. Their set-up was unusual in that one photographer stood behind the camera, while the other scrutinised the 'footage' from a connected laptop on a tripod. Each time the shutter clicked, the photographers would notoriously huddle by the monitor to discuss and adjust the models or props for the next still. 'They understand how to communicate their ideas to each other with few words,' a fashion industry insider explained, 'almost like a secret language.'

Their highly stylised photos, while immediately recognisable to fashion followers, weren't to everyone's taste. Fans of traditional film photography were less keen on their use of digital cameras and the pair's heavy manipulation of each image in post-production. 'Their pictures tend to be luminous, as though the subjects were lit from within, and to feature odd backgrounds, stark contrasts, and rich colour,' a fashion magazine explained. 'The models' flesh and hair can appear to be made of plastic. Many of the images have a staged, formal quality, like the nineteen-thirties Hollywood photographs of George Hurrell, but with a sheen that suits the video-game age. At times, the models seem almost synthetic, and in some respects they are, because Mert and Marcus do a great deal of post-production work. They are known for manipulating their pictures. They shoot digitally, and then alter the images on a computer screen.'

The photos for Jamie's Armani campaign were no exception, and both he and Sasha appeared in a set of sharp, black-and-white photos with a hint of 1930s art deco to them. Jamie oozed masculine charm as he posed in immaculately tailored suits which looked almost liquid, dripping sensually off his well-honed physique thanks to the photographers' use of digital enhancement.

His co-star Sasha, with her high cheekbones and slicked back hair, was Jamie's perfect match, looking breathtakingly sculpted against the fluidity of her white, flowing dress. It was already an electric setting, and Jamie and his Russian colleague – who had just been ranked second in the international women's Top 50 Models list – also had much in common. Like him, Sasha had never dreamt of being a model. She was studying art history at the Russian State University for the Humanitites when a friend and photographer took her photo and gave it to top modelling agency IMG in 2005. Ranked as the world's number one model management firm with offices in New York, London, Milan, Paris and Sydney, they also boasted a host of famous faces on their roster, including Heidi Klum, Tyra Banks, Jamie's friend Lily Aldridge and his former campaign co-star Gisele Bündchen. Sasha had been snapped up straight away and, as had been the case for the Irish male model, bookings came in thick and fast and she hadn't looked back. Four years later, as she posed opposite Jamie in the 2009 Armani campaign, she had already done a six-season run for Prada and had a string of high-profile adverts to her name.

So it was little surprise that the dynamic duo were an instant hit when the Armani adverts launched six months later. Fashion blogs were inundated with literally thousands of critics in support of the stunning pair and it was starting to look like every campaign Jamie touched turned to gold. 'I think that what makes a good ad campaign is the combination of everything: the models, the clothes, the photography and effects. In this case, for me, this campaign is perfect,' one fan gushed. 'Mert & Marcus shoot the BEST campaigns EVER! PERIOD! I love this campaign. I'm so glad Jamie Dornan was chosen, he complements Sasha wonderfully,' another posted on a forum dedicated solely to the new Armani adverts. Someone else proclaimed, 'Oh Sasha, how I love thee and Jamie is so hot!'

Further adoration was just around the corner when hot on the heels of this Armani casting, Jamie got a call from his agent at Select to say that Calvin Klein had been in contact again and they wanted him back. It was to be his third casting for the trendy fashion house and Jamie was overwhelmed with the offer.

This time the bigwigs inside one of the world's biggest fashion houses wanted Jamie to star with gorgeous actress Eva Mendes in not just one, but two campaigns: Calvin Klein Underwear and Calvin Klein jeans. Jamie and his 'Dornan Furrow' had already acquired a reputation for producing excessively steamy shots with his female counterparts but this campaign was to be so raunchy that his renowned sexy poses with Gisele and Kate Moss would pale in comparison.

Jamie couldn't wait to get started and was excited to meet his famous Hollywood co-star who had well-respected film credits to her name, including recent hits *Hitch* and *The Women*. The brunette had also just been voted the most desirable woman of 2009 in a poll by website *AskMen.com* and when Jamie met her in the flesh, she was no disappointment.

The location was equally as impressive; Jamie and Eva were flown first class to Palm Springs in California for the week to shoot the no-expense-spared campaign. The lavish resort, which boasts year-round sunshine, stunning landscapes and its own beach, had long been a luxury playground to the rich and famous and made an incredible backdrop to the shoot. Once there, Jamie and Eva were met by world-renowned photographer Steven Klein, who had been hired by Calvin Klein to work his magic.

One of the most influential fashion photographers of his generation, Klein was famed for his risqué iconic images of a string of stars, including Brad Pitt, Madonna, Justin Timberlake and Naomi Campbell. Klein had a way of persuading stars to pose for intensely private and erotically charged images, and this particular photo shoot bore all the hallmarks of his legendary snaps. Jamie and Eva would be required to star semi-naked in the black-and-white photos, with the male model at one point cupping the actress's bare breasts. Wearing just Calvin Klein underwear, Jamie would also have to climb on top of the beautiful star, lying pressed up against her for minutes at a time – not easy when that someone is a stranger and a beautiful one at that. Moreover, the pair had been smothered in oil by the make-up team so that their skin glistened for the photos, thus making for some amusing scenes as they tried to climb into different and sometimes very intimate poses.

Thankfully for Jamie, Eva was friendly and approachable – better still, he fancied her and the on-screen attraction was electric. 'We were in Palm Springs, we had a whole week of it and it was outside and there was sun. We actually had time to get to know each other and she's really very nice,' Jamie said afterwards.

Single and bowled over by her natural beauty, the model was simply in awe of the actress. For Jamie this latest signing meant that he was getting ever closer to his dream of acting, since he played out the part of her on-screen lover while Klein captured every intimate move. 'Eva is incredible – as you see her on the screen, so she is in the flesh. She's great fun to be around, very sexy. I'd say she's the template for how every woman should look,' he gushed afterwards.

There was no mistaking the chemistry and Calvin Klein couldn't have been happier with the result. Jamie too was impressed and clearly overwhelmed by the prestige of the campaign. 'Calvin Klein Jeans and Calvin Klein Underwear are both such iconic American brands that to play a part in these campaigns is a true honour,' he said at the launch. 'Working alongside the sensationally sexy Eva Mendes on both shoots was incredible.'

Thousands of black-and-white shots were taken by enthusiastic Klein, as the pair performed perfectly for the camera. By the end of the week, the legendary photographer had a hoard of incredible images of the duo in a huge variety of sizzling poses, including one with Eva rubbing her bare body against Jamie and another with the actress suggestively stretching her long legs over him.

The autumn campaign of 2009 was building up to be huge, with ads scheduled to appear everywhere from billboards and bus stops to magazines and newspapers the world over, including spreads inside American titles *Lucky*, *Elle*, *GQ*, *Vanity Fair*, *W*, *Nylon*, *Details*, *Interview* and *InStyle*. When the ads hit the news stands, it became clear that twenty-seven-year-old Jamie's latest fashion campaign would be going down in history as one of the most controversial yet. 'Is Eva's new Calvin Klein ad too revealing?' *The Insider* questioned as it hit the mainstream press. 'In a pic for the underwear ad, Eva is seen cuddling model Jamie Dornan, who only wears white undies,' another explained. 'Then, in another shot for the jeans ad, she is snapped getting topless. Her breasts are only covered by Jamie's hands. Is it just too much?' The *Daily Mail* moaned, 'It's more proof that fashion houses are pushing boundaries to extremes in order to get publicity.' Judging by some New Yorkers' demand that a sixty-foot billboard of the duo be pulled down immediately, the answer would be a resounding 'yes'.

City chiefs were bombarded with complaints after the ad,

showing Eva draped across Jamie with a hand on his tight-fitting pants, was pasted on the entire side of a building at a busy intersection in the city. While drivers stopped to admire the spectacle, residents claimed the board was 'too rude for public consumption', particularly as it could be seen by children, and demanded that it be taken down. Carl Wilson, a worker from Queens said, 'Some of us don't want to expose our kids to something like this – it's borderline pornography.' Critics also claimed that the picture suggested she was about to whip off his underwear and it was 'out of place' in such a prominent location. 'It's absolutely disgusting,' another blogger wrote. 'Not everyone wants to see this kind of fornication on their way to work in the morning. Someone needs to get in touch with Calvin Klein and get them to take it down, now.'

Jamie's co-star Eva was adamant that there was nothing wrong with the ad and slammed the critics, insisting her steamy pictures with Jamie were 'beautiful'. Pointing a finger at those who were unhappy, she said, 'It's a religious group that has a problem with the image [...] That's what I love about this country. We can voice our opinion and beliefs like that. But they're wrong. I don't think I'm traumatising any children. I think it's a really tasteful and beautiful ad.'

For every hater, there was an admirer and Jamie's friends were firmly in the latter camp. But while they were impressed with his latest job, they had ample material for some serious ribbing. 'His mates call him up and tease him, there's no way Jamie will be getting an ego about this anytime soon,' a friend revealed. 'They see him writhing around with a famous actress looking all serious and brooding on a billboard and the night before they were knocking back pints of Guinness together in the pub. He takes it well and enjoys the normality of it.'

His relationship with Calvin Klein was tight and Jamie found that they were giving him more and more work. In what was another positive step towards getting more screen work, the model snapped their offer to be the face of their new scent CK Free, which involved starring in a mini TV advert.

Jamie was flown to the famous Silurian dry lakebed in Baker, California, in scorching heat, along with Fabien Baron – creative director of CK Jeans – to put together the one-minute commercial short. The pair got on brilliantly as the filming got underway on the dry, desert-like landscape which seemed to spread out for miles.

In the romantic scenes, Jamie is seen driving a Mustang across the plains at sunset before getting out of the car with his arms outstretched and staring down the lens of the camera. It was a scene that was replicated by Jamie years later with his wife on their honeymoon, but for now the model was just acting out a fantasy.

The public reaction at the time was good but was even better in 2013, when he was announced as the lead role of Christian in the *Fifty Shades of Grey* movie and the videos were revisited by excited fans on YouTube. 'Honestly he is Christian – he's been real this whole time and yes they found him for us,' fan Sabrina Beaucage wrote. 'This is the real Christian Grey, he's such a peach, you can tell Jamie is right for this massive film role. He will do it justice,' penned fan Maxine Wilkie.

Jamie himself was pleased with the result; he clearly enjoyed the chance to act and do more than just pose for stills. 'Fabien's amazing. His mind is incredible. He's a creative director, a stylist, a photographer, he can kind of do it all. And he's really fun at the same time and a joy to work with,' he said. 'Calvin Klein are good at just letting me be me and not turning me into something else. I didn't have to change and a lot of guys that you see in campaigns have just been taken off and look like a puppet. It's funny because modelling was never something I wanted to happen to me,' he added.

Whether Jamie wanted to or not, though, his modelling career was now a serious business and so lucrative that he had to make it a priority; preserving his good looks and keeping his physique toned was essential to keeping clients happy. Much to the astonishment of many colleagues, he openly admitted that he loathed going to the gym and had no fitness regime to speak of. Begrudgingly, Jamie had to start adopting a series of tried and tested exercise workouts to keep himself trim, which he squeezed in during quiet spells while on shoot. 'There's a lot of hanging around so I use any downtime to work on my arms and core with variations on press-ups and crunches,' he told *Men's Health* magazine soon after the Calvin Klein campaign. 'It really is about press-ups every day. I'll aim to do about fifty in the morning and loads more throughout the day.'

Nevertheless, the heart-throb model still had an appetite for high-calorie meals and junk food, including BLT (bacon, lettuce and tomato) sandwiches and an ongoing penchant for hamburgers and fries. 'I love a dirty burger,' he admitted, 'the kind where the ketchup and mayonnaise goes all over your face. That and a lot of ale. I don't watch what I eat, I don't understand how guys can do it. Food is so good, and if you feel bad about what you eat, go out for a run. I am obsessed with burgers as soon as I check in somewhere it's "I'll have a bacon cheeseburger with fries", and I won't talk to anybody until I'm satisfied and I've eaten the burger and then only then will I call them up and say "right, let's meet up!"'

He clearly wasn't shy about his 'non-diet' diet and his rider for one magazine photo shoot included 'one bacon sandwich, one British Roast Chicken on wholemeal, one King prawn and smoked salmon baguette, a bottle of water and a Coke to wash it down with'.

There was no time for wearing kid gloves in Jamie's life – he wasn't going to be precious about preserving his good looks; life was for living, as his mother and father's cancer battles had taught him. Wild nights out drinking with his mates, surfing and some extreme ski holidays were all the order of the day, as nothing was going to stop Jamie from having a good time. 'Work hard, play hard' had clearly become something of a mantra for him.

However, a taste of the good life came at a cost on one snowbound mountain break when he suffered a horrendous injury in a terrifying skiing accident. An accomplished skier, Jamie was out on the mountainside when he lost control and smashed into the ice. Doubled-up in excruciating pain, hospital medics discovered that he had shattered his shoulder. Treatment was complicated and after enduring an astonishing four years of constant pain, Jamie went through a host of therapies to fix the broken bones, including two operations using keyhole surgery.

Jamie had always been insecure about his looks; he didn't understand why the fashion industry thought he was so attractive and now lifting weights and doing push-ups left him in agony. Keeping fit was one way in which Jamie could take control of the way he looked and, for once, he would have liked nothing better than to hit the gym. 'I have massive insecurities about how I look and will do for the rest of my life,' he said. 'I'm amazed if people are happy in their own skin. I see someone and I think, "F**k him, look at him, he's got way better arms than me."'

Even though he was one of the best-looking men in the public eye – and his position in *Cosmopolitan*'s Top 10 hunks proved this point – Jamie couldn't understand how people could end up so vain, spending hours in front of the mirror preening. It just wasn't in his make-up. 'I've never understood that "my body is a temple s**t" although mine does help to pay the mortgage,' he said some years later.

There was further frustration for Jamie, as he couldn't stand it when people assumed that he was unintelligent and uneducated solely because of the way he looked and his job as a male model. It had reached a stage by then where his notoriety was affording him an outstanding quality of living but Jamie was becoming fed up with the price he had to pay for that: being treated like something of a village idiot. Nothing could have been further from the truth and the prejudices he faced almost daily were clearly making him anxious. 'People assume you're stupid enough as it is. Then you take your shirt off and they're like, "He must be an idiot." Seriously, people approach me and you can see it in their eyes. They speak to you very s-l-o-w-l-y. They're like: "Let's talk about grease and oil on your body. And aftershave. And your grooming technique." I understand. I mean, if I saw a picture of me, I'd probably be the same.'

The reality is that he was a privately educated doctor's son, who adored reading, playing golf, going to the theatre and skiing with his well-heeled pals. He had very few links with those inside the fashion industry, except to turn up to a photo shoot or promo – both of which were so brief that there was no time to make any firm friends. 'I don't really have any model friends; I have people that I kind of know but we don't go out and talk about fashion over like an ale,' he laughed during an interview with Nylon TV. 'It's not really a profession. Some people actually say they are just a model but what do you actually do? It takes up so little of your time.'

Going on to speak about where he'd really like to be, he added, 'Every great character has already been played and played really well so you're kind of waiting for that remix where they're going to recast it with some skinny Irish guy – like Steve McQueen say.' Jamie was clearly desperate for a credible acting career and pronto. The glamorous assignments hadn't seen him resign himself to a future in modelling but instead had shifted his focus further from fashion to movie roles.

Luckily, and thanks to relentless auditions, the much hankered-for parts had started to trickle his way, even though he wasn't going to take the easy route. Jamie knew that it would be all too simple to worm his way into the acting world by going for the roles of 'lover' or 'boyfriend', for which his career as male supermodel had already perfectly typecast him.

Unsurprisingly, nearly a decade in the fashion industry had ensured that he was fed up of playing the handsome co-star in various fashion campaigns, and being a piece of on-screen eye candy was not on his agenda. 'I'm not going to take my shirt off every time I'm in front of the camera. It's very accessible. Google "Jamie Dornan Torso" and there you are. I've done it enough that I really don't see how it's interesting anymore.'

Thankfully, and much to his relief, he finally secured the movie role he'd been waiting for – that of a scruffy tramp. Jamie's agent had called to say that after a surprisingly successful audition, he had won a part in small-scale British independent movie *Shadows in the Sun*, and it didn't require him to look pretty. Instead, the role was an interesting one. Jamie was to play Joe, a troubled man who lives like a vagrant but is looking after an elderly widow living in a remote house on the Norfolk coast, by bringing her cannabis to ease the pain of an illness.

It was just the break he'd been looking for, as it was completely different from the sexy roles he'd been up for previously. Set in the 1960s, the part was gritty, as Joe was a mysterious loner who was sleeping rough on the beach inside an old shipwreck. Jamie was to grow a scruffy beard for the role – a breath of fresh air for the model who usually spent hours with a team of stylists making sure that he looked immaculate for the camera. 'It was an amazing film to be part of. It's a very quiet little film, it's not going to create too much of a stir. It's set at the end of the sixties and I was able to grow a big beard for the part which I enjoyed having. I kinda miss it. I would like to grow it back again but I'm not allowed because of Calvin unfortunately.'

But best of all, the movie afforded him the unique opportunity to perform opposite eighty-year-old acting legend Jean Simmons. One of Hollywood's brightest actresses of the 1950s, Jean's career spanned decades and saw her act alongside Hollywood greats Burt Lancaster, Kirk Douglas, Victor Mature and Marlon Brando. The gentle family drama was to mark her return to the big screen and was sadly to be her last ever film. Working so intimately with Jean was a dream come true for Jamie; while clearly being star-struck on meeting the legendary actress, he quickly felt at ease with her, as her down-to-earth nature meant that they soon managed to form a firm friendship. They became so fond of each other, with Jamie realising he had much to learn from the star, that they kept in touch after filming finished. 'I'm not sure what they were expecting, some Diva from Sunset Boulevard perhaps,' said the two-time Oscar nominee, who grew up in Cricklewood in Essex before moving to Hollywood. 'I like to think I've always kept a sense of reality. I think that's down to my family and especially my brother whose attitude about me was always, "Oh good, the kid is working",' Jean said of her time on the film.

Jamie found the stories that she regaled to him and his co-star James Wilby deeply fascinating, particularly those of legendary actor Marlon Brando – one of his all-time heroes. 'In a perfect world I would play Stanley in [Tennessee Williams's play] *A Streetcar Named Desire*,' Jamie had once said of his dream role, 'but that can't be touched; Brando did it and I don't think they should ever re-do *A Streetcar Named Desire*.'

Working alongside one of Brando's contemporaries left him ever more certain that a career in the movie industry was for him. 'Jean was, what, seventy-nine when I worked with her? And when I think of all the films she was in, and how thoughtful and generous she was,' he said. 'I have to be careful here, because I was almost gonna tear up. She started as a kid. She had so many great stories. She worked with Marlon Brando and Frank Sinatra – in the same movie! I'm sure she got sick of me asking her about that. She told me one of her first jobs was as Vivien Leigh's stunt double. They rolled her up in a carpet and threw her into a pool for a scene where Vivien was to be drowned. She said she stayed underwater for what to her seemed like forever, but when she came up, she knew it was only a few seconds. She laughed about it, then she went from that to starring in *Spartacus* [1960]!'

The movie in which Jamie and Jean were now starring hinted at a time-defying romance between them despite the age gap of fifty-five years, which amused rather than embarrassed the model-turned-actor. 'I did fall a bit in love with her actually,' he admitted to the *Evening Standard* newspaper some years later.

Even after filming ended, the unlikely pals vowed to stay in touch and Jamie went for lunch at her home in Santa Monica several times before her death in January 2010, a year after the movie's release. 'She was one of my favourite people in the world,' he added, 'and it was a huge loss when she slipped away. *Shadows in the Sun* was her last film and she was the most incredible person. I kept in touch with Jean – she was hilarious, and had the spirit of a twenty-one-year-old right up to her final days.'

In so many ways working on the film had made a lasting impression on the young starlet and when it got a thumbs-up at its premiere at the Dinard British Film Festival, he was both thrilled and relieved. Its release in UK cinemas, however, brought moderate success and reviews were varied. '*Shadows in the Sun* unfurls as quietly as a mouse and could be accused of lacking urgency and bite. But it is well played, particularly by Simmons who still has the charisma of a star turn,' a write-up in the *Evening Standard* newspaper read.

Keen to keep up the momentum and wanting as much experience as possible, Jamie also agreed to appear in two shorts. Supporting young director Will Garthwaite with his 2009 slice-of-life *Nice to Meet You*, Jamie agreed to play a man being chased by police who begs a woman to hide him after jumping into her back garden. She agrees and the sexual chemistry between them is obvious, even when he finds himself at the centre of a love triangle after sleeping with her daughter. Starring Sting's wife Trudie Styler and her real-life daughter Mickey, the twenty-minute film, which sees the woman take revenge by calling in the police to arrest him, was less an example of Jamie's acting abilities and more an illustration of the society crowd he was mixing with at the time. It clearly wasn't the proudest entry on his acting CV and when years later a journalist asked him about his role in the film, he said incredulously, 'I can't believe you watched that!'

In a similar vein, the wannabe Hollywood star played the lead role in an award-winning short from the 2009 London Film Festival, *X Returns*. Although the twenty-minute caper attracted little long-term attention, it did at least give Jamie the chance to hone his acting skills and star alongside beautiful *Neighbours* soap star Holly Valance. A film critic noted at the time, 'Well filmed but it seemed more like a trailer for a feature film than a short in itself. Still, how can one not enjoy anything starring Holly Valance?'

Jamie had clearly been welcomed into the London TV and film crowd, and was being invited to a host of events and red carpet premieres in the broadcast calendar. One outing at the 2009 BAFTA awards party caused a stir amongst the gossip pages of the British press when he was seen chatting up *Harry Potter* star Emma Watson. Friends of the pair claimed the 'face of Dior' was determined to woo his way into the teenage actress's affections. 'Emma has no shortage of admirers and Jamie is one of them,' a friend told the *Sunday Mirror* newspaper the following week. 'She's a bit of a romantic so he's had to do it the old fashioned way and lavish her with chocolates and flowers […] He isn't used to girls saying "no" to him so he will keep trying. When he meets her at the next showbiz bash he will try again […] Last time all the guys were making moves on Emma so Jamie knows he has to be a bit quicker.'

Meanwhile, his modelling career remained a success and being the on-going face of Calvin Klein was starting to become a label he couldn't get rid of, even when he might have wanted to most. 'I potentially did too much modelling – it's detrimental. Do enough big, high profile stuff and it's not just, "He got his photograph taken". You become part of a brand. With Calvin Klein that was me. So there's a danger that it's in too many people's psyches. I think I'm going to be constantly battling that label,' he explained.

Although it may have sounded big-headed, Jamie was far from it. In the same month as the CK Free advert was released, Jamie agreed to a rare interview with the *Daily Mail* newspaper, and the real man behind the good looks and rippling torso was revealed for all to see. 'The guy who is paid to just be pretty is also the sort of chap you'd like to have a drink with – if only he wasn't going on to a party in his capacity as the face of Calvin Klein's new fragrance, CK Free,' the journalist noted. 'He describes CK Free as being for "guys of a certain age who are able to let loose and do what they want before they're tied down" which makes Jamie an excellent choice.

'Hot model Jamie is single, he is chronically shy, he is sharp and he is level-headed. So if you're a normal woman who likes normal men and fancies the one they call the Golden Torso, do track him down.'

But could Jamie remain 'normal' and 'level-headed' forever? He'd done well to keep his ego in check thus far but with Hollywood calling with some major roles just around the corner, surely it was just a matter of time before his inner diva was unleashed?

Chapter Eleven

ONCE UPON AN ACTING CAREER

'You spend a few years as a model, leaning against walls and looking depressed while someone takes a photo of you, but God forbid you can also act. I'm not saying that I'm a good actor, not for a second. But this idea that there's no way you can do both – well it's always going to bother me and it's something I'm going to fight!'

Although Jamie had indeed put in a tireless battle over the years to achieve a bona fide acting career, with every audition his agent had put him forward for, he had taken another hit to the ego. Jetting to Los Angeles for auditions during pilot season had been one of the most 'dehumanising' experiences of his life and despite hundreds of read-throughs for TV and film roles, Jamie didn't feel he'd benefitted much from the experience. The expert model had instead resigned himself to the fact that he wasn't going to get any better at undergoing the terrifying process of auditioning in front of casting directors. 'I'm still not one of those people who are good at auditions. Even after I got my first acting job, thanks to Sofia, I still went a while without working. If you ever wonder why some actors end up taking shit jobs, it's because they have to pay the mortgage – or because they just want to work.'

Jamie was desperate to make acting his trade and finally in 2011 he had the massive breakthrough he'd been dreaming of since leaving school at eighteen. He had won a part in a high-profile American TV drama. Some ten years after striding out of his family home in Holywood with a promise to his family that he was going to achieve his childhood ambition of being an actor, glory was his. Jamie had walked into the audition room and impressed immediately. The job was his and the Dornans were both thrilled and relieved for him.

Jamie knew how lucky he was to land such a coveted role, realising he could have followed in the footsteps of thousands of other wannabe actors before him who had spent years playing mediocre parts. He, at least, had scored just a handful of small roles while still gaining worldwide fame as a model, before hitting the big time. 'Being in LA for pilot season you read some really, really awful stuff. I could have very easily ended up in something rubbish,' he said. 'I find it hilarious when actors are like, "Yeah, I just read the script and thought I had to do it." You just get lucky if you get in something good and then you try to pass it off that it was your plan.

'You'll be in some audition room with a casting director for some bad, bad film and you see some quite famous actors' audition tapes for that same project. Then they'll end up in something independent and classy that gets nominated for some award and then they will act like they would never go up for something like that; but they actually did, they just didn't get it.'

Jamie's own 'lucky' break meant that he could at last put his modelling career behind him – forget it even. 'I've been quietly looking for a way out of it for a while,' he admitted to a magazine at the time. 'I'm trying to categorically say that I don't want my photograph taken any more.'

Jamie was to star in US TV series *Once Upon A Time*, created by the much-lauded writers Edward Kitsis and Adam Horowitz of hit shows *Lost* and *Tron: Legacy*. Unlike his history of audition flops, Jamie had instantly impressed the dynamic duo. 'The minute we saw Jamie, we loved him and thought, "That's the guy",' Kitsis said. 'He's very talented.'

He was to play the part of Sheriff Graham in the fairy-tale drama screened on ABC, who would later materalise as the Huntsman from Snow White. Based in the fictional seaside town of Storybrooke, Maine, the show's plot revolved around its residents who were characters from fairy tales transported to the real world and robbed of their memories by a curse.

Instead of worrying about being typecast as the Calvin Klein model playing the role of the show's heart-throb sheriff, Jamie excitedly took up the challenge; it was an interesting concept, the script was gripping and the cast was impressive. 'I got lucky with *Once Upon A Time*. That was the first job I did when I committed to being an actor. Before that it was just something I did now and again and got enjoyment out of it,' Jamie explained.

Showing once more that he had taken his first steps on the

rung of the celebrity ladder, Jamie joined social networking site Twitter, where he was soon to converse with fellow stars of the show. Just before jetting out to Vancouver in Canada for the start of three months of filming, down-to-earth Jamie tweeted: 'My last Sunday in London before heading to Vancouver for "Once Upon A Time". Mixed emotions.'

On arriving on set in the picturesque town of Steveston in nearby Richmond a few days later, though, any pre-filming nerves were quickly allayed after meeting the cast and crew. Famous Brit actor Robert Carlyle, star of blockbusters *Trainspotting* and *The Full Monty* – who played Rumpelstiltskin in the series – quickly became a firm friend. 'Bobby's a legend on every level. You know a great actor when it's all so effortless,' Jamie said of his newfound friendship with Scottish actor Robert Carlyle. 'We bonded quickly – a lot of people from Belfast and Glasgow do because they're similar places.' The close-knit cast also included Hollywood actress Ginnifer Goodwin as Snow White, Jennifer Morrison – famous for her role as Dr Allison Cameron in TV show *House* – as bondswoman Emma Swan and Josh Dallas, who took on the role of Prince Charming. The latter became good friends with Jamie, as the pair tried to outdo each other on collecting 'followers' on Twitter. 'I'm in competition with @joshdallas for number of twitter followers. He's beating me, which is unfair because I'm a slightly better guy,' Jamie wrote before jokingly re-tweeting a fan's reply: 'He's a great looking guy but you are so much cuter, just sayin'! @JamieDornan1.'

For Jamie, with no drama school experience to draw on, it was a plunge in the deep end but he was learning quickly on the job. He had a measured on-screen quality, having honed a style of acting from watching films, in particular Hollywood stars Al Pacino and Robert De Niro in movie favourites *The Godfather* and its sequel.

Preferring their 'less is more' approach, his modelling career had also made him master of the long, lingering look and Jamie's 'Dornan Furrow' was now creeping onto the small screen. 'I don't want to be showy. I'm not interested in that and I don't want to do it,' he said of his style of acting.

It was a huge learning curve for the handsome clothes horse and Jamie embraced the gritty role, particularly the challenge of flitting between the two sides of his character: that of sheriff and the Huntsman. 'He's a bad ass, he's a pretty mean guy and as it transpires he's been raised by wolves and has had very little human contact and has very little understanding of humans and only has respect for animals,' Jamie said of the complex role. 'The joy of this show for many of us is that we do have two characters to play and that you're conscious of the other one constantly; when you're playing one you're thinking of the other one.'

Co-star Jennifer Morrison was also taken with the show, citing that *Lost* fans would be taken with the plot, which she explained as: 'Basically, it's as if every fairy-tale character ever written is real and actually exists, but they've been cursed and they don't know their true identities. They are living in our reality not knowing who they truly are. And because [of that], they're never going to have their happy ending.'

Jamie also felt true job satisfaction during dramatic scenes opposite Lana Parrilla, who played the town's mayor Regina and counterpart the Evil Queen. 'If you're a vulnerable character and you're standing up against something and having your say then that feels pretty amazing. My character is the victim of bullying by the Evil Queen and everyone wants to stand up to their bully. Rarely do you get the opportunity to do that, so I've enjoyed those scenes where I've got to put her in her place,' he said.

As if *Once Upon A Time* hadn't given him enough opportunities already, it also meant the chance of working with a wild animal – a wolf – another plus for his future acting CV. 'The wolf was amazing to work with although I was little allergic!' Jamie tweeted. 'It's been a real eye opening process, I've never worked with a wolf before […] we've been quite lucky with him but sometimes he's hungry and he's grumpy and he's bored and he doesn't want to stay on his mark but don't we all, we often don't want to do that, so why should a wild animal!?' he added in an interview.

Despite fourteen-hour days with regular all-nighters, Jamie was enjoying the three-month shoot in Canada and settling into life of a jobbing actor well. 'The weather in Vancouver makes Ireland look like Florida,' Jamie noted on his Twitter page soon after arriving, before admitting a few weeks later, 'Another cracking day on set of Once Upon A Time with Jen Morrison, Lana Parrilla and a lunchtime set visit from Ginny Goodwin #ilovemyjob.'

A month into the project, Jamie was starting to miss London. He tweeted: 'Eight hours time difference can be a killer! Need Rugby World Cup to start to take my mind off it. #homesick'.

Exhaustion was also beginning to creep in, as he admitted:

'Been shooting for 13 hours today on #onceuponatime. Still another scene to do! And same again tomorrow. Exhausted. Employment's tiring!'

However, all that hard work was worth it. When the series premiered in America in October 2011, it netted ratings of 12 million a week. It also garnered thousands of devoted fans – and not just for the show but for Dornan too. It may have looked initially as though Jamie had been typecast as the show's eye candy but many were as impressed with his acting skills as his good looks. 'Thank you all for your kind words! Don't stop watching #onceuponatime. As I've said before ANYTHING can happen in fairytale land! X' Jamie tweeted as the show was being aired. 'Made it to over 10,000 followers! Bizarre stuff. I probably know 17 of you. The rest, I thank you, and I'm sure you're lovely.'

Even copycat versions of the leather jacket he wore in his role of Sheriff were flying off the virtual shelves of online clothing stores. Jamie's role had been written in for seven episodes and no one was expecting such a backlash when his character was killed off by the Evil Queen, with many of his newfound devotees taking to the internet to complain. 'I miss him in every episode. Graham/Huntsman was an awesome character. None of the new characters have made up for the void that is having no Jamie!' one fan wrote on YouTube. 'Why do the hot guys have to die in this show? Jamie Dornan was my favourite,' blogger Jessica Standen wrote on a fan forum. Another wrote, 'Now that magic has been brought to Storybrooke they have to find a way to bring Graham back. I mean these are the writers of LOST we are

169

talking about. They do whatever the f*** they want and I want this pretty man back on my TV every week!'

'I really do like that show on ABC #onceuponatime but I just feel that there was something missing in the last episode,' Jamie teased on his Twitter page as the eighth episode of the series was aired.

'By the way, I AM still in Once Upon a Time. I'm now @Jared_Gilmore (Henry)'s body double. I do all his stunts. Honestly,' he added as his fans started to complain of his absence.

Jamie had become a household name and a stream of press followed, with magazines and newspapers clamouring for one-on-one interviews to which Jamie occasionally agreed. 'Model-turned-actor Jamie, 29, is starring alongside Robert Carlyle in US fantasy drama *Once Upon A Time*. So we cosied up in bed (where else?) with the hot Northern Irish lad,' an interview with *The Sun* newspaper proclaimed.

'Love from the fans is flattering. That's what makes the show. They are so essential to everything involved with *Once Upon a Time*,' Jamie said. 'If I have them on my side, that only can be a good thing. I'm not going to take all the credit; Graham's a well-written and interesting character. The reaction to Graham's death … I'm pleased that people are so concerned, but I don't think we need to be calling the FBI or anything.' In fact, fans' concerns over Jamie's untimely death in the hit series had now taken a bizarre and sinister turn, and the executive producers and show writers Adam Horowitz and Eddie Kitsis had even started to receive hate mail and death threats for writing him out. 'I think death is a big deal, obviously. Killing off a main character is something we did with Sheriff Graham (Jamie Dornan), and I still get death threats about that,' Kitsis revealed. 'I think people can be pretty hairy from what those boys tell me [Adam Horowitz and Eddie Kitsis] I don't want to induce any sort of hatred or anything and I don't want those guys to be massively under fire from, you know, crazy fans because of what they did. But it wasn't solely their choice. But I guess, I should essentially take it as a compliment that people care that much. A bit of hate mail's OK, but the death threats – that's too much,' Jamie said of his fans' extreme behaviour.

Jamie was a hit and the producers, not wishing to ignore the public outcry over the sheriff's demise, wrote him back into a series of flashback scenes. His first reappearance on the show would be the following year in the season finale episode 'A Land without Magic'. 'Hope everyone in the states watches the season finale of 'Once upon a Time' tonight. It's a goodie,' Jamie wrote to his Twitter followers as he made his return to the show.

The show was so popular that UK broadcaster Channel 5 had bought the series and a month earlier had premiered *Once Upon A Time* to a healthy audience of 2 million.

Success on home turf was important to Jamie and the show's writers again admitted how important he was to the cast, promising that he would be kept on the roster as a guest star for as long as Jamie wanted. It was an enviable position for any actor to be in. 'I would say there is definitely a chance of his coming back,' Kitsis confessed soon after Jamie's one-off return to the show in 2012. 'He may be dead in the present, but he's alive in flashbacks, and we would love to see him back all schedules permitting.'

Such praise from two of the TV industry's greatest writers could well have turned Jamie into an overnight diva. However, regular visits home to Belfast and London, and staying in touch with childhood friends ensured that the model remained incredibly grounded. Free time away from the camera saw him indulge in stag dos abroad, nights out in London's Soho on whisky tasting sessions with old school friends and frequent visits to New York. 'My friend hairstylist Harry Josh holds a brilliant birthday party every year at the Gramercy Park Hotel, New York. My best nights are always in NYC,' Jamie admitted.

The heart-throb model was also in continuous contact with former bandmate David Alexander, who was giving a music career a second shot. In support of David, who was now headlining solo shows in top London haunts Notting Hill Arts Club and Ronnie Scott's, Jamie had started to backtrack on his views about his short-lived foray into music, which he had previously described as 'terrible'. 'I've pulled the reins in on that a bit, because there were other people involved,' he told *The Scotsman* of his time in Sons of Jim, 'but I didn't have a lot of belief in my personal capabilities. I essentially wasn't fulfilled by it, but we had some good times. I would do a lot of different things differently if we did it again.'

Also, although Jamie was starting to get noticed out and about, much to his great joy the times were still few and far between. 'Two girls just walked by me in street. Girl 1 (whilst pointing at me) "Is he cute?" Girl 2 "No, he looks like a creep." Erm I can hear you!' Jamie admitted to fans on Twitter. 'In a cafe. Was asked my name for the order. I said "Jamie" they said "okay Jimmy" I said "no it's Jamie", they said "oh Jerry!" I said "fine".'

Even when judging a Calvin Klein underwear competition in London, Jamie was clearly managing to go incognito, as a scout from his own modelling agency pulled him off the street and asked if he'd like to take part in the Europe-wide contest to find the next male model. The prize was a luxury trip for two to South Africa and a year-long contract with Select. 'They stopped me outside TopShop and thought I could enter this competition. They thought I could probably make this whole look work. Poor girl she said: "I'm from Calvin Klein, would you like to model underwear" I said "no" and she said: "please, go on, it would be great" and I said "erm no, no, no" and she chased me down the street and gave me her number but alas I didn't enter!' he described.

Life was good for Jamie and never more so than when he was back in Belfast. His father Jim and stepmother Samina had built a comfortable family home together and Jamie, along with his two sisters, made regular trips back there. Returning to Belfast, particularly for St Patrick's Day and, most importantly, Christmas – a family occasion with 'a lot of seasonal Guinness' which Jamie had never missed – was a chance to catch up with loved ones and recuperate. It was also helping to keep the model-turned-actor grounded. Jamie tweeted soon after finishing the *Once Upon A Time* shoot: 'Home to Belfast to find my Dad's added a putting green to the house. Very pleasing! #noplacelikehome.'

Family was indeed incredibly important to Jamie; in fact, of all the successes in the past few years, family matters were the most important and becoming an uncle had been his proudest moment of all. 'One of my sisters is expecting her first child, that's the most exciting thing in my life at the moment, to be honest. I'm going to be the best uncle in the world, that's the plan anyway. I can't wait,' he told the *Evening Standard*.

His father Jim was also proud of becoming a grandfather for the first time and admitted that, despite having delivered thousands of babies, having a new child born into the family was something really special. 'I don't really feel like a grandfather I feel more almost like a brother, which sounds ridiculous but I just enjoy the children so much,' he admitted a few years later, 'and Samina is really enjoying our granddaughter Delphine and of course she's a genius, she can count to twenty and she's not even two yet!!'

As Jamie approached his thirtieth birthday in May 2012, it was a good time to reflect on all he had achieved in his life. 'I'm really excited while I've loved every second of living in London during my twenties I've got more acting lined up and I'm fulfilled professionally and personally,' he admitted in that year.

Most importantly, under the radar – and despite a spectacularly busy work schedule, a burgeoning new career as an actor and a busy social life mixing with Hollywood's rich and famous – Jamie had fallen in love. Three years before, the actor hinted that he had finally found someone special, telling a newspaper: 'I'm definitely not single. I'm in a pretty serious relationship actually.' While it was early days back then and having nurtured the relationship away from the public eye, Jamie was now certain she was 'The One'. But who was this leading lady in his life? And would she really turn long-standing bachelor Jamie, desired by millions of women across the globe, into a happily married man? Only time would tell, but things in the romance department were certainly looking promising.

Chapter Twelve

FALLING IN LOVE

Amelia Warner is breathtakingly beautiful. Jamie was introduced to the actress by friends on the LA scene during a trip to Tinseltown in 2009 and by all accounts it was a match made in heaven.

Amelia was a popular, well-established actress with a string of TV and film credits to her name, had a secret penchant for reading 'the classics', was a talented musician, loved eating delicious high-calorie sandwiches in hidden-away cafes and, crucially, loved a pint of Guinness. She couldn't have been more perfect for the hamburger-obsessed, music-mad bookworm that was Jamie Dornan.

Their similarities were numerous. Amelia had first-hand experience of the darker side of fame, having dated and 'married' Hollywood star Colin Farrell as a teenager. Not unlike Jamie's relationship with actress Keira Knightley, Amelia had endured her fair share of crazed fans, intrusive paparazzi and being the 'plus one' on red carpet events during her year-long romance with the Irish actor.

Jamie and his new love interest, it was fair to say, were certainly not going to be the kind of couple who courted fame in the celebrity sense. The duo had also endured similar hardships in their careers, particularly as they both shared a dislike and fear of the LA auditioning scene.

At the time of their first meeting, the Calvin Klein model was still a novice at the ruthless pilot season where hundreds of actors flood to Hollywood each spring to audition for the latest parts on offer. The pretty Londoner, meanwhile, had been through the mill for almost a decade; she had landed her first movie role at seventeen and was pretty jaded by the whole process too. She wasn't the only Hollywood star to hate the annual tryouts; *Miss Congeniality 2* actress Leslie Grossman, said of it, 'The process of trying to land a part in a pilot can be exhilarating, heart wrenching, thrilling, stressful, devastating, heady and hair-raising to name only a few of the emotions they inspire. Imagine a bunch of wild animals that haven't eaten in a year and someone throws a big raw steak in front of them. That's pilot season to actors.'

Hardened to the constant competition, rejection and uncertainty of the acting game, Amelia admitted that her only way of coping was to quash every competitive bone in her body. 'I'm ambitious, but not competitive. You'd drive yourself crazy if you were. You know, there are actually enough jobs out there for all of us,' she said four years before meeting Dornan. 'I don't even really want to talk about how I hate LA. It's so English to hate LA. I'd like to say I love it, but I don't. It's such a weird place. If it were my choice, I wouldn't spend a day there.

'Everything shuts at eleven. And everyone thinks they're so crazy and wild and liberal and they're not! So much work goes on there, but so much s**t goes on there, too.'

The UK – and specifically London – was clearly where her heart was and coincidentally Amelia had grown up as an only child just ten minutes from Jamie's pad in Notting Hill, in west London. Like her new model boyfriend, she loved spending weekends browsing through the bric-a-brac and vintage clothes of Portobello Road's world-famous market and having dinner at one of Jamie's favourite nearby haunts, the Electric Diner.

Their childhoods, however, were poles apart. While Jamie's idyllic upbringing was spent in a sprawling, two-parent family home in a leafy suburb of Belfast, Amelia was raised by her single mother – actress Annette Ekblom – on a Ladbroke Grove council estate. Following in the footsteps of her mum, who starred in the original West End cast of *Blood Brothers*, Amelia was involved in youth theatre as a teenager – just like Jamie – and was noticed by a scout while performing in a school play. 'I began acting at school in Herefordshire and I always liked it, though I didn't necessarily think I'd do it for a living. My plan was to go to Goldsmiths College to study History of Art, but someone saw me in a play at school and told me that I should meet this agent,' she told *The Telegraph*. 'I started to get work and so I deferred my place at university.'

A string of roles in UK television productions followed,

including *Kavanagh QC*, *Casualty*, *Waking the Dead* and the BBC miniseries *Aristocrats*. Hollywood soon came calling and Amelia starred in the US feature film *Mansfield Park*, alongside Lindsay Duncan and Jonny Lee Miller, and in the Hallmark Production of *Don Quixote*, with John Lithgow and Bob Hoskins.

In 2000 she starred in the BBC adaptation of R.D. Blackmore's *Lorna Doone*, where she played the lead role of Lorna; later that same year, at the age of seventeen, Amelia was cast as a child bride who gets corrupted by the Marquis de Sade in hit movie *Quills*, starring Geoffrey Rush, Kate Winslet and Michael Caine.

Despite starring alongside so many Hollywood greats – an incredible achievement for such a fresh-faced schoolgirl – acting had left a bad taste in her mouth. In fact, mirroring Jamie's feelings towards modelling, she knew that the film business wasn't her true calling. 'I was thrown into the deep end but I hadn't expected any of it,' she said of her high-profile role in *Quills*. 'It was overwhelming and when I was on set it was the moments when my scene was being filmed that I disliked it the most.

'To be an actress felt wrong; I don't know why that was. I thought I was so lucky to have the work but was never happy.'

Amelia's twelve films after her first small part in *Mansfield Park* in 1999, where she played a teenage Fanny Price, also included playing Charlize Theron's sister in sci-fi thriller *Æon Flux* in 2005, when she was twenty-three. Then, in 2008, at the age of twenty-six, and a year before meeting Jamie, she gave it all up. Fed up with being 'thoroughly miserable' as an actress, the pretty starlet decided to pursue a music career. It was something she had always dreamed of, claiming that singing and songwriting had always been integral to who she was and citing film scores as one of her biggest influences. 'The constant pressure of having to prove myself as an actress didn't sit well with me. I got fed up with acting because my heart was never in it. I'd be in LA auditioning in front of thirty people. The feedback that I always got was that I didn't want it,' she explained. 'I was up against lots of actresses who would fight tooth and nail for a part but I didn't have the passion. I didn't want to suffer through the moments of nervousness. I felt exposed and judged all the time. So I thought it was best to get out.

'Music is my soulmate but that's what stopped me from doing it for so long. I felt like if I get judged on this that would be devastating. But at least I have the passion to get through it.'

Under the name 'Slow Moving Millie' – a joke between family and friends who had always known her as 'Millie who wanted to be a professional musician' – Amelia spent two years forging ahead singing, playing the piano and songwriting. 'I spent so much time figuring out what I wanted to do that the name Slow Moving Millie is a joke because I am so slow to work it out. Having been an actress, this felt like a different part of me. It is a separate identity,' she described.

The idea of all that inevitable public scrutiny that went with being a famous actor was also a massive turn-off for Amelia, who had experienced it first-hand during her whirlwind, year-long love affair with Irish star Farrell when she was just a teenager. The couple met at the premiere of her movie *Quills* in September 2000 and got engaged soon after. However, the duo made world headlines when they secretly married on a beach in Tahiti, only to split four months later. Serenaded by ukulele players and with 'no family invited', the marriage was completely sensationalised in the press, including reports of how Farrell had tattooed her nickname 'Millie' on his ring finger.

Thanks to Amelia wanting to set the record straight, though, it later transpired that the union wasn't legally binding. 'We didn't actually get married – it's not actually true. I think we've been too polite to deny it. We had a ceremony on a beach in Tahiti that was by no means legal and we knew it wasn't. It was just a thing we did on holiday. We went shark feeding and then we did that. We booked them both on the activities desk at the hotel,' she told *The Sun* newspaper some years later. 'It really wasn't this secret wedding that no one was invited to. It was lovely, it was silly, it was sweet but by no means was it a serious thing and I think my mum thought it was quite funny.'

Amelia dumped the actor in November 2001 and both were heartbroken. 'I loved him so much,' she told *The Observer* newspaper several years later. 'I had the most amazing times of my life with him. He was a fantastic partner. I would have married him for real. But we were too young. I had stuff to do and he had stuff to do.' Farrell was equally devastated: 'I was madly in love. Jesus, it was a whole thing. I asked her to marry me. I had a ring. There was a time I thought I'd spend the rest of my life with this girl. That time didn't last that long, and that was that.' Soon after their split, Farrell became known as something of a Hollywood 'bad boy', filling his days with *Playboy* models, sex tapes, cocaine-and-whisky binges and rehab.

Amelia's mother Annette clearly didn't think Colin had been a bad influence; in fact, he had clearly charmed his way into her affections when dating her daughter. 'I don't recognise all this stuff I am reading about Colin at the moment. He never used to swear and behave like that,' she told a newspaper after the split, when Farrell was making headlines for his bad behaviour. 'In fact, when he was with Amelia he was very sweet. He was from a nice family and was a lovely young man, polite and well behaved. I can only assume that his "bad boy" behaviour is to do with his career, which seems to be taking off. He is probably putting it all on.'

Not that Amelia would ever have needed protection, it seemed; behind her sweet, angelic exterior lurked a feisty and fashionable girl-about-town, who at the age of twenty-two was bold enough to tell a newspaper that she had bought all her friends vibrators for Christmas. 'I think every woman should have one. I can't believe they haven't already. They always say: "Oh no, I couldn't possibly buy one for myself. But then, if someone else were to get me one",' the then actress divulged.

By the time Jamie came across Amelia, she had blossomed into a more sedate – still stunningly attractive – incredibly talented musician by trade. 'She is beautiful – delicate waifish build, with vast and decadently lashed eyes, an auditorium-enchanting smile and skin all luminous and brilliant like the moon; she is poised, a touch grungy, a touch princess,' one gushing critic once said of her. 'The beaaautiful actress and songstress is shy, charming and downright talented. Her music is hauntingly beautiful,' a music blogger proclaimed in 2010.

Whatever Amelia's first impressions of handsome Jamie, it must have seemed funny to think that he, meanwhile, had been recently compared to her famous ex, since he was being touted within the film industry as the 'new Colin Farrell'. 'He's Irish, dark-haired and can grow great facial hair, so he's being promoted as the next Colin Farrell' the *Mail on Sunday* claimed.

Jamie and Amelia's union couldn't have come at a more exciting junction in their lives. Both had finally found direction and, indeed, had undergone something of a job swap: Jamie had chosen to be an actor, desperate to forget his short-lived career in Sons of Jim, whereas songstress Amelia boldly admitted that she never wanted to act again. Their past experiences in notoriously difficult professions would certainly have helped them to sympathise with each other as they tried to get to the top of their chosen careers.

While Jamie had landed his first big TV role in *Once Upon A Time*, Millie's music career had also taken off. In July 2009 she had written and performed the song 'Beasts' for a Virgin Media TV commercial and a second single, 'Rewind City', had also been used for another advert for mobile phone giant Orange. In October 2011, Amelia had finally achieved 'the dream'. She had been signed by Island Records ahead of the release of her cover version of The Smiths' 1984 B-side 'Please, Please, Please, Let Me Get What I Want', which had been selected as a soundtrack to the John Lewis Christmas advert for that year.

By 2011 they had also set up home together, as Amelia had moved into the Notting Hill house that he once shared with his father, Jim. Despite their relationship being kept under wraps, proud Jamie clearly couldn't contain his excitement for Amelia and wrote on the social media network Twitter: 'All in the UK, get on I tunes or get to record store and buy "please please" by the wonderful Slow Moving Millie. Out today. @Missmillieuk.'

Two months later, Amelia released her first studio album, 'Renditions', which included ten 'chilled out' covers of 1980s hits. The collection of tracks was chosen as Amazon's Album of the Week and, although it was well received by reviewers and music lovers alike, it only reached eighty-nine in the UK charts.

Her Christmas single, however, made the Top 40, reaching a peak position of thirty-one. Amelia was over the moon. 'When I got signed to Island Records it was a relief. It was scary walking away from a job that was making me money. I was scared I'd regret it – but this has proved to me that it wasn't crazy to throw it all away,' she said at the time.

Another of Amelia's recent decisions – to move in with Jamie – had also proved a success and it was obvious to all and sundry that they were a couple deeply in love. A two-week trip to Los Angeles, where Amelia was writing her album, saw the pair indulge in a few of their shared passions, including a Dr. Dog gig, visiting old friends in the city and 'a proper American breakfast of pancakes and crispy bacon' in a diner. The Californian city had become a second home to the pair where, as Jamie confessed, they tended to spend half the year 'drinking, playing table tennis, bumming around' blissfully undisturbed by his impending celebrity status.

Family ties were still strong and Jamie continued to make regular visits home to Belfast, often with Amelia in tow, whose down-to-earth nature would have been a hit with his dad and stepmother. Jamie's much-loved older sisters Liesa and Jessica – one working for Disney and the other mother to two babies under the age of three – were still close at hand, too, living in London and Cornwall.

It was a blessed life indeed and back home in London Jamie and Amelia enjoyed nights in watching trash TV, with Amelia 'loving' *The X Factor* and Jamie admitting to watching *The Real Housewives of…* series on Bravo. 'My enjoyment of "Don't Tell The Bride" is worryingly slipping from ironic to genuine…time to turn off the TV,' Amelia tweeted in 2011.

The pair also shared a love for Elvis and a memorable, if not unusual, night out for the couple towards the end of that year was seeing crooner Engelbert Humperdinck perform at London's Royal Albert Hall. 'It was a really random night, but I had the best night, it was amazing. He had his shirt unbuttoned, he had a fan on him, in between songs he told jokes and stories about Elvis and Marilyn Monroe. He was incredible,' Amelia recounted in an interview. 'The Man, The Legend, Engelbert Humperdinck. Cannot say enough. What a hero!' Jamie tweeted the following morning.

Intimate details of their two-year relationship were also offered up to online blog *The London Chatter* by Amelia, who painted a picture of comfortable days in and cosy nights out with 'my love' aka Jamie Dornan. 'I'm not a huge fan of the cocktail so [a drink out] would have to be a pint of Guinness at The Coach and Horses in Soho with some lovely friends,' she revealed. 'Date night would be spaghetti pomodoro, red wine and candlelight at The Ripe Tomato on All Saints Road with my love. Brunch is at home with the papers, Bloody Marys and my friend Markus's home fries. Secret place – Cork and Bottle, a very old fashioned wine bar hidden and tucked away under the craziness of Leicester Square – perfect for a late dinner.'

The following year saw a romantic trip to Paris and a joint 'obsession' with the Olympics, which were hosted in London. Jamie seemed particularly enthralled as the Olympic flame passed by their London house and admitted that he would be watching the Games avidly on TV.

Another big step for the duo saw them buy a second home in the Cotswolds: a rural retreat in the Oxfordshire countryside popular with the rich and famous, including model Kate Moss, Liz Hurley, Lily Allen and Hugh Grant. Picture-perfect and an ideal place to raise a future family, 'it's to get away from London at the weekend,' Jamie said of the cottage in 2012, 'so that's two mortgages.' For the model-turned-actor a countryside hideaway was perhaps justly needed. Having struck lucky with his *Once Upon a Time* role, Jamie had also landed a part in gritty BBC2 drama *The Fall*, and this time he was to play the lead. Despite this and being on the cusp of worldwide fame, though, Jamie was adamant that the paparazzi wouldn't be interested in their life. 'I'm a thirty-one-year-old not twenty-one. I don't leave clubs at 5 am. Who would be interested in a nerd like me? Honestly, when I hear that I'm cute and charming I feel like a French bulldog,' he said. 'My level of fame,' he added in another interview, 'has no impact on my life.'

It was true to say that, aside from their two homes, everything about the couple was distinctly 'normal', with not a hint of living like the stereotypical Hollywood stars. 'I despise extravagance. I do not fly a private plane. I do not have bodyguards and I do not buy branded stuff. I have a house, two dogs, a watch. That's good enough for me,' Jamie told Polish *Glamour* magazine.

He also loathed the idea of being famous, as did Amelia, who by 2013 had undergone another career change after her music career had fizzled out. She had now achieved another childhood ambition of opening a clothes shop. Called 'Found and Vision', and selling vintage 'fashion, furniture and finds', the store was popular with fashionistas and A-listers alike, such as Kate Moss, Sienna Miller, singer Florence Welch and London IT girl Mary Charteris. It was handily located just around the corner from their Notting Hill home. 'Found and Vision is one of London's infamous vintage boutiques. Set in the heart of Golborne Road, the boutique is awash with treasures from Ossie Clark to Lanvin,' *i-D* magazine raved.

Amelia, who had loved fashion and the Bohemian-esque area of Kensal Rise ever since moving there aged four, seemed as happy and personally fulfilled as Jamie, who was taking great strides in his acting career. She had also been welcomed with open arms into the Dornan family and a future together seemed unquestionable.

True to form, Jamie proposed and much to their loved ones' delight their marriage day was set for 27 April 2013. It was to be an intimate wedding at trendy retreat Babington House in Somerset, surrounded by close family and friends.

The country house hotel – an offshoot of London's media

hang-out Soho House – was a popular wedding venue with A-listers thanks to its privacy within eighteen acres of British countryside and an eighteenth century chapel for the ceremony itself, followed by a luxury champagne wedding reception in its critically acclaimed restaurant. Couples who had previously married at the stunning retreat included comedian James Corden and Julia Carey, Fat Boy Slim and Zoe Ball, and Amanda Holden and Chris Hughes.

With the day set and preparations underway, Jamie, who had recently endured months of filming, enjoyed a much-needed break with his future bride. Four months before the April nuptials, the pair splashed out on a sun-kissed beach holiday in Miami. The couple were seen playfully cuddling in the sea, with Jamie in red trunks and Amelia looking striking in a white triangle bikini and her dark hair tumbling over her shoulders. 'Jamie and Amelia are clearly a couple in love, they couldn't keep their hands off each other while swimming in the sea together. Both were tanned and beautifully turned out, they're the kind of couple glossy magazines would be fighting over to have grace their pages,' an onlooker remarked.

It was just as well the couple had grabbed a break while they could, as the lead-up to the wedding was fraught. A week before the marriage, Jamie was in the thick of a massive publicity drive, as the smash-hit crime drama *The Fall* was due to launch on BBC2 in a month's time. Jamie was winning rave reviews for his portrayal of a doting father turned psycho killer in the chilling series and just when he was hoping to wind down for the biggest day of his life, press requests were coming in thick and fast. 'We meet Jamie Dornan the week before his wedding,' a journalist for the *Sunday Times* wrote. 'His wayfarers and phone are on the table. Just 31 he is currently appearing in his first BBC drama. Family must be next – it's all coming together for the former model.'

Indeed, everything seemed to be happening at once. Jamie had spent the evening before the *Sunday Times* interview writing his wedding speech in a diner on Portobello Road and had burst into tears. Although a big day in any groom's life, for Jamie it was going to be particularly emotional. While he had finally found the girl of his dreams, the woman who raised him, his beloved mother, wouldn't be there to witness it. It was also a unique chance to bring all those he loved and cherished together in one place to celebrate his love for Amelia; as well as dad Jim, stepmother Samina and sisters Liesa and Jessica, eight of Jamie's groomsmen were his friends from back home. 'Holywood is where my heart is,' Jamie admitted.

His childhood pals had already done him proud with a two-day stag do in Berlin. Determined to give Jamie the perfect send-off from bachelorhood to married man, all nineteen of his invited friends went on a beer bike, which involved pedalling a mini pub on wheels around the German city while 'knocking back barrels of beer'. It was a 'brilliant craic', as the actor admitted afterwards.

When Jamie and Amelia's big day finally came around, the setting couldn't have been more perfect. Coincidentally, the nuptials were held just two weeks before Jamie's ex Keira Knightley wed Klaxons singer James Righton in a romantic ceremony in France, which was splashed across the world's press. Thankfully for Jamie, his big day went by virtually unnoticed, despite the attendance of a clutch of TV celebrities such as his *Once Upon A Time* co-stars Ginnifer Goodwin, Josh Dallas and Jennifer Morrison.

Once they were husband and wife, and following the weekend celebrations, Jamie and Amelia immediately set about achieving another all-time dream: a honeymoon driving across America in a convertible Mustang. In a five-week 'honeymoon to end all honeymoons' the newly-weds drove from California to New York in a scene right out of the CK Free advert he shot in the year they met. The romantic trip saw Jamie drive 6,000 miles – 'We were taking our time to do it,' he later admitted – with highlights including driving through the West Virginia mountains and visiting Graceland, the home of Elvis Presley, which for the actor was 'a dream come true'. 'It was like a movie, it did feel like that at times. A convertible Mustang makes a lot of sense when you're in California but less so as you head further East!' Jamie told breakfast TV show *Daybreak* on his return. 'You know you grow up just wanting to do that kind of trip and a few people said, "Oh you'll regret it if you don't go and lie on a beach for two weeks," but you can't do this forever if you know what I mean, this was a once in a lifetime thing.'

It was a welcome break from months of hard slog but even on the open road, Jamie couldn't help thinking about work, particularly since his new show *The Fall* had premiered while he was away. 'It was strange being away with the first three episodes of *The Fall* coming out though,' he said. 'No one likes to bother you on your honeymoon but I was thinking, "It's been on for thirty seconds and no one's been in touch".'

The honeymoon period continued back home in London and Jamie's wife was a hit – everyone who met them seemed to be enchanted by her charm and beauty. Actress Bronagh Waugh, who played Jamie's wife Sally Ann in *The Fall*, said, 'I introduced myself to Amelia saying "You're the hot wife, I'm the not-so-hot wife." She's just lovely, he's very lucky to have her.'

'Jamie is absolutely besotted with her and so are we all,' a friend of the newly-weds said, 'she is literally the most perfect person imaginable for him.' What would make their life together even more complete was a family and a few days before his wedding, Jamie admitted that he was ready to take on the challenge of fatherhood. 'I want to have all that. I'd say I'm pretty ready, I want to experience it when I'm still young,' he said.

Nothing seemed to be out of Jamie's grasp and behind closed doors not only was a baby on the way but a Hollywood film career playing a certain Christian Grey was in the making too. For the time being, though, the actor had his first major TV role to promote and finally, thanks to playing the part of a cold-blooded killer, Jamie was thrilled to see that his pretty-boy model image had been turned on its head for good. Even his wife, home from their honeymoon, was left traumatised after watching him in one particularly gripping episode of *The Fall*. 'My wife hadn't seen the third episode so we watched it together [after the wedding]. She was a little bit wary of me for about half-an-hour after it finished,' he said. 'I had to win back her trust.'

A friend of theirs also admitted that she felt uneasy in his presence after watching the show. 'It's the last effect I want from a friend, but I'm glad,' he said. The reaction was praise indeed and Jamie was justifiably proud of himself; *The Fall* had been exhausting, psychologically challenging and one of the best experiences in his thirty-one years of life. And, like everything, it seemed that he hadn't quite expected it…

Chapter Thirteen

A KILLER DAD

'I auditioned to play a smaller role in "The Fall", a detective. I never think auditions have gone well, but with this one I actually did think I did a good job. Then I didn't hear anything for a couple of weeks.' Baffled by his misjudgement, the model-turned-actor decided to try his luck elsewhere and jetted to Los Angeles for pilot season. He had booked himself a hire car and apartment at the other end and was bracing himself for a month of thankless auditions. However, as soon as he landed in Tinseltown, he got an excited call from his agent saying that the BBC wanted him back in London right away to read for a different part. 'That usually means it's some really tiny, insignificant part, but it was completely the opposite, which never happens,' Jamie explained.

Writer Allan Cubitt, known previously for award-winning TV series *Murphy's Law* and *Prime Suspect*, had seen Jamie's first audition and wanted him to try out for the lead role: a grief counsellor turned serial killer called Paul Spector. The crime drama set in Belfast – a co-production for RTE and the BBC – was already being earmarked to be a hit by excited TV critics. Jamie was gobsmacked by the offer. 'Then the fear sets in. Do I take offence that whatever I did in the room, trying to play a detective, they saw the serial killer in me? Is that a compliment? Then there was the proper fear – I'm going to get fired at the table read, and they'll realise they've got it completely wrong,' he told the *Sunday Times*.

It was a complex role and Cubitt, along with the show's producers, which included Belgian director Jakob Verbruggen – who had worked on US drama *The Bridge* – needed to be certain that they hired the right actor for the job. In the five-part series, Paul Spector works as a grief counsellor by day, hiding behind the façade that he's the perfect family man: a dad-of-two and a devoted husband. In his other life, as he sketches grisly images in a diary and hides his butchering tools above his daughter's bed, Spector is stalking the streets of Belfast, plotting and carrying out the gruesome murders of professional women.

Whoever was going to fill the role would have a challenge on their hands, having to convey two completely different characters in one. 'Paul Spector was a conundrum,' one newspaper explained. 'We saw him strangle women in the night then make his two young children breakfast in the morning. He would hover in doorways and slip through windows to attack his victims a terrifying figure who loomed over the screen and would then settle into an armchair and offer bereavement counselling at work a few hours later, sometimes without having been to bed in between.'

The checklist for casting Spector also included employing an actor who could star opposite actress Gillian Anderson, as she had already landed the role of detective. Best known for her long-standing character of Special Agent Dana Scully in sci-fi show *The X Files*, her character in *The Fall* – DSI Stella Gibson – is sent to Belfast to solve Spector's high-profile murder case. Therefore, finding someone who had an acting style to compliment hers was key. 'Gillian was first choice for the part of detective. She is extremely minimal in what she does, very internalised, very thoughtful, very unshowy,' creator Cubitt explained. 'So I knew I needed someone who could match that.'

While there had initially been pressure on the show's producers to cast a bigger name than Dornan for Spector, Cubitt went against the grain and argued that it was more important to have someone the right age, since statistically most serial killers are in their late twenties. Within minutes of Jamie walking back into the audition room, Cubitt knew he was the right man for the job. The casting panel had chosen a scene where Spector, who had returned back home from a voyeuristic burglary, goes to his children, whom he had left alone and asleep while his wife worked a night shift as a nurse. Much to the room's delight, Dornan's interpretation was chilling. 'Some people were playing it as if he wanted to murder his child but Jamie came in and spoke very kindly to the boy, then kissed his daughter goodnight, and that's more disconcerting for the audience,' he explained.

Although Jamie may have wanted to forget his years of

modelling in the acting studio, they had clearly taught him some essential skills, such as being able to portray a feeling and emotion solely through his face and body language. As the old proverb goes, 'a picture paints a thousand words' – Jamie was master of communicating a whole range of emotions to his audience with just one powerful look. He was measured and poised and although Cubitt realised that he had struck gold, he now had to convince the people further up the chain that this ex-model was the right choice. 'I had in my mind someone who is very still in what they did and who the audience would project quite complex feelings to. Jamie had that quality where he was watchful where he didn't reveal very much about himself and bit by bit you were drawn into trying to decipher what sort of person he was,' the writer explained.

Even Jamie was stunned at how sinister he looked when he later watched himself playing the killer on screen. 'Everyone in the process of casting me must always have seen that darkness in me. Yet I'm not sure I even saw it myself. Basically, it must have been inside me, which is kind of worrying,' he said.

For Jamie, it was a dream role and the script was one of the best he'd ever read. It wasn't long before he was told that the part was his. He was in good company too, along with Gillian Anderson, Bronagh Waugh – best known for playing Cheryl Brady in Channel 4 soap *Hollyoaks* – who was to play his on-screen wife SallyAnn, and Irish actress Laura Donnelly, who had been cast as a female solicitor targeted by the killer.

Jamie was sent the script and even before the shock of landing the part had worn off, he started working on developing the character. 'I thought I was in over my head when they cast me. It was tough, really tough, and not an easy place to have your head in,' he told the *Radio Times*. 'I was all "time for the fun to start. Let the research begin. Let me only start reading about unspeakably horrific men."'

Jamie focused on round-the-clock research into psychopaths, as he tried to get inside Spector's mind. He started reading books, watching films and digging out interviews that would give an insight into how a cold-blooded killer thinks and operates. As days turned into weeks, it was clear that Jamie's preparations for the drama were starting to have an effect on his psyche. 'I didn't read anything other than innocent death and it does affect you, big time,' he said. 'It's not a good mindset to be in for any real length of time.'

But Dornan wasn't complaining and despite the grisly research process, now more than ever he knew that becoming a serious actor had been the right choice – it was everything he had dreamed of. 'I woke up one morning just before we started filming and on my chest were all these books about murderers. I was going to bed reading about these horrible people and of course it affects you […] It was a very strange process but I loved it, I really loved it – I'm not sure what that says about me.'

Dornan quickly found that there was one real-life killer that stood out as the perfect inspiration for the role. Ted Bundy murdered more than seventy women in America during the 1970s, mostly thanks to his ability to win their trust with his looks and charisma. At one point, he was killing one woman a week, all the while maintaining a steady relationship with his girlfriend, socialising with friends and working on the campaign trail for congressmen. Like Spector, he inhabited two entirely different personas before finally being executed in 1989 after confessing to murdering over two dozen women. It was a crucial observation that helped to shape Jamie's role. 'I've approached Spector as two completely different characters which made it easier for me. He's either in killer mode or family mode, but neither is easier than the other,' he told BBC Belfast in a behind-the-scenes interview.

Jamie had spent hour upon hour avidly watching interviews with Bundy on YouTube. Despite being a brutal rapist and necrophile, the good-looking killer carried a certain magnetism, a 'quality' that Jamie thought would work for Spector. Bizarrely, he also talked about himself in the third person, which Dornan found compelling. 'It's fascinating watching him because he's super charming and good-looking. He ran two Congress campaigns in the US, was a super-bright law graduate, had a long-term girlfriend, a normal group of friends but he's a psychopath. So these people do exist!' Jamie said of his research. 'Bundy talks about himself in the third person. He was handsome and the people around him had no idea what he was going to do. This guy was seriously charming and so articulate.'

The handsome star had started to sketch out exactly who Spector was and how he perceived the other people in his life, particularly the difficult-to-unravel relationship with his children. Although Cubitt didn't think Spector was capable of loving his son and daughter, Jamie decided to make him even more sinister by showing that he did, which in return revealed an unexpected human side to him. 'What is creepy about that is the normality of it all. He's a grief counsellor, of all things. He has a wife and two kids that I think he loves. I think Allan would say that Spector's incapable of love and therefore doesn't love the kids. I would try to argue that slightly.

'I would say that he portrays a certain form of love, certainly to his daughter. In a way, I don't think Spector's that bad of a husband. I think he shows good qualities, despite the fact that he hunts and kills innocent women. It is all quite sordid. But I want to show how regular these guys can be,' he told *Interview* magazine.

In what would have been a shock to many of the show's viewers, Jamie even went so far as to try to find something he liked in Spector, believing it was important for an actor to learn something from his character. 'For Spector, despite all the horrendous acts, there's something that I'm fond of in his character, and I think a lot of those characteristics in him that I admire, he uses for quite odious purposes. I wish I had his attention to detail, and his efficiency,' Jamie confessed.

With research done and dusted, the four-month film schedule started in March 2012 and he flew to Belfast, leaving girlfriend Amelia back home in London. Although a bag of nerves, worried that on the first day of filming he wouldn't step up to the mark, the Northern Irish star was at least happy to be back in his home town. The model-turned-actor decided to rent a flat in the city centre, even though his much-loved family home in Holywood was just a few miles away. Apart from the punishing schedule, meaning that he would have little time to relax, Jamie also didn't think it appropriate to be living with his obstetrician father Jim while spending his days playing a killer. 'My dad delivers babies, can you imagine?' he told *Interview* magazine. 'I've spent all day strangling women, while Dad's bringing a new life into the world. I can't deal with that!'

Being back in Belfast, though, meant that he could easily meet up with old school friends and go to the pub in the evening. It was good to be back and it was to be the longest time he'd spent back in Belfast in a decade. 'I had an apartment in the middle of town for three months. And I've never actually lived in Belfast because I grew up just outside, so I experienced the city on a different level, waking up and going to get coffee and read the papers on my day off. I'd never done that, so I just loved it. And it's nice to not have to repeat yourself, as well, in terms of your accent,' he joked to *Red* magazine. 'I made the decision quite early on not to live with Dad during filming, because of my schedule I couldn't just come home and have a cup of tea. I needed to be on my own. But it's brilliant meeting up with my old mates from home we just talk football and it's a terrific release from the intensity of the shoot,' he added in an 'on set' five-day diary for the *Daily Mail*. It turned out to be a wise decision, since Jamie was struggling to clear his head at the end of the day. 'There'd be times where I'd see my mates, they'd want to go out for dinner and I had to say, "look, I can't do it, I need to lie in a bath and listen to Maria Callas and think about 'happy'."' he said.

It had already been a steep learning curve for Jamie; arriving on set for the first time, it was a relief to notice that for once in his life he wasn't there to look pretty, 'cute' or even vaguely decorative. He was there to play a brutal killer and being a former underwear model played no part in it. However, far from revelling in the moment, Jamie was wracked with nerves, convinced that he'd be discovered as a fraud and instantly fired. 'In my first speaking scene I was thinking, "OK this is it, they'll be firing me now. There was nothing in my C.V. that warranted me being there,"' he said.

Jamie was startlingly talented and although the cast and crew were immediately awestruck by his character portrayal, he wasn't fooling anyone: he was new to the acting game. 'Every day that we did something horrible, I'd say, "I'm sorry this doesn't come easily to me,"' Jamie admitted.

It wasn't an easy role to play but pulling on Spector's 'killing gear' – a 'commando-style catsuit' – for the murder scenes certainly helped, although entering the killer's mind, and what felt like his body, made Jamie feel sick. So lost was he inside the role that even watching the show back was excruciating, particularly the family scenes where Spector remains a devoted dad. 'It's discombobulating when you're filming it, I find it sick. Then I find it hard to watch, the proximity of the two existences, killing someone then picking up my child and putting her to bed. I struggled with it; it's you doing it. It feels like you're doing it yourself … okay, you're playing a character, but it's still sickening,' he explained.

Already feeling the intensity of being Spector on set, Jamie refused to adopt the 'method' technique of acting where actors draw on inner emotions and experiences to portray a character and 'live' inside their mind twenty-four hours a day, seven days a week – even when filming finishes. 'I just don't think it would have been healthy to try and stay in character or that mindset,' he said. 'I don't think I could do it, that method and run away with it? Jesus. I just made a point of switching off.'

It was the killing scenes that Jamie felt were the hardest, with some so harrowing that he felt moved to apologise to the actresses who played his victims. Working on such tough material, on very dark, atmospheric sets, Dornan was also keen to lighten the mood whenever possible by dancing around the set between takes. 'When it was appropriate I would make someone laugh. There were scenes where I've got a ligature around my victim's neck and I'm pretending to squeeze with all my life. She's foaming at the mouth, my sweat's dripping in her eyes, I'm watching her die and her eyes are bulging. After every one of those scenes, when they'd say "Cut!" I was saying, "Oh my God I'm so sorry. I'm going to untie your feet here. Is that OK?" Because I am not that guy. I did my best to slip out of it as soon as "cut" was called.'

While the psychological strain was tough for Jamie, he also experienced searing physical pain portraying Spector's fitness regime and fight scenes. Two operations, including keyhole surgery, on a smashed shoulder from a skiing accident four years previously had left the star in constant agony. His sex scenes, though, were a breeze in comparison for the former supermodel, who was clearly now a dab hand at stripping for the camera. But for *Hollyoaks* actress Bronagh Waugh, his on-screen wife, getting naked in front of the gorgeous former Calvin Klein pin-up – along with a roomful of cameras and crew – was terrifying. So terrifying, in fact, that she turned to drink before takes. 'He's a body of a god and I'm a normal girl,' she said. 'It was our first full nudity scene for Jamie and me. We were both really nervous. The director Jakob Berbruggen is from Brussels and he was so very European about it all. I had to get into a bath and I was begging, I mean begging for bubbles. I was "Please whack in some Radox!" but the director said it would spoil the shot – and he was right.'

However, stress turned to comedy when her modesty patch – a strip of nude-coloured material, which is stuck to an actor's private parts – started floating off as she lay in the hot bath. 'I had this modesty patch on my lady bits and all actors will tell you they are notorious for not working very well. In the scene Jamie is watching me getting into the bath and I'm closing my eyes sinking into it. When I opened them the plaster was floating up and down in the path,' the down-to-earth actress remembered. 'Jamie was looking and we were just wetting ourselves. I think it is the grossest thing that has ever happened to me. Jamie's seen me naked so many times he said "Bronagh I'm really over it."'

On the other hand, when it came to Jamie's first-ever full nudity scene, which was shockingly graphic, even the experienced underwear model knocked back whisky to get through it. 'There was an incredibly graphic sex scene outside. It was very cold so we both had a wee dram before it,' Bronagh told the *Sunday Mirror* newspaper. She also admitted that the whole experience was far from romantic: 'It's so weird as you get to know someone, I don't see him like that (romantically). You get nervous with any sex scenes – you feel awful.'

A measure of just how famous Jamie had become came when his co-star Aisling Franciosi was completely overwhelmed on first meeting him. Playing the Spector family's babysitter who falls for the attractive father's charms, the pair had a number of scenes together. She said of acting opposite the former Dior model: 'Part of me was telling myself that I had to be professional but another part was screaming inside. My first scene was one where his character came to my bedroom, it was intense. But he was great, very supportive. He's a humble guy.'

Jamie was clearly a hit with his fellow cast members and while there were plenty of high jinx on set, he made sure he stayed out of their way once filming was over for the day. 'I felt they probably wouldn't want to spend any time with me,' he told the *Daily Mail* newspaper. 'I apologised after every take, it was like a release to apologise and then we'd have a laugh. I used to beg for someone to make me laugh.'

He and Gillian Anderson also made a mutual decision not to meet each other socially, since they were playing the hunter and the hunted and thought it would increase the tension on set. 'Because of the nature of the show it wouldn't have made sense to hang out together. The more we kept apart the more sense it made.'

As it turned out, the on-screen pair did very little filming together and appeared together only four times. They both admired each other's work, though, and stunning actress and mother-of-three Gillian told him in an interview with *Red* magazine, 'I think it was pretty clear from the beginning that you were the man for the job. I just think it was a matter of convincing the powers that be. I've been in the same situation before, with people fighting my corner, but having to convince studios that you're the one – it takes some effort.'

It was certainly worth the effort and Jamie found he was

learning quickly on the job, even though there was no denying he was a complete natural. Without even realising it, Jamie used his hands to show what side of Spector's complex character he was portraying at any one time. 'I wasn't aware of it at first but the way I used my hands became a way for me to play Spector's awareness,' he told *Interview* magazine. 'You see the difference in how he deals with the family, with his kids and the way he approaches things in his life.'

Jamie, who had previously admitted his method of acting came from watching Al Pacino in *The Godfather*, could also be seen adopting his long silences and lingering, pensive stares. 'I've played a lot of broken people, maybe the silences are about the different kinds of vulnerability in them,' he explained.

Jamie's own emotional side was also being tested to the brink and he admitted to crying to let out pent-up emotion. The demanding role also caused him to wonder how his nearest and dearest would react to seeing him embody such a terrifying man. 'I think it helps that I'm quite open and I'm a crier. Spector is devoid of emotion.

'It will be interesting to see what the reaction is [by friends and family] because it is dark, I surprised myself with how dark I looked at times; I think I looked – not pleasant,' Jamie said shortly before *The Fall* was aired.

Having filmed the glossy drama out of sequence, Jamie had the chance to watch it back in order before it was released for broadcast and he was immediately struck by how horrifying it was. 'When you see it all put together I do struggle. I understand why people find it difficult to watch,' he said.

Just under a year from the show's wrap, *The Fall* premiered on 12 May 2013 on Irish channel RTI and the following evening on the BBC, to an admirable 3.5 million viewers. It went on to become BBC 2's highest-rating drama launch in almost a decade, thanks in no small part to Jamie's sickening portrayal of Spector.

TV critics and viewers were equally captivated and revolted by the series, and internet forums sprung up overnight devoted to Jamie, his cast members, show spoilers and plot twists. 'If it had been a plot by Dornan to kill off his pretty boy alter ego overnight, then it was a stroke of genius,' one journalist reported. 'Well done Jamie, you've more than proved your mettle as a serious actor and not just a bit of fluff who once appeared on the arm of Keira Knightley,' wrote Maeve Quigley in the *Sunday Mirror*, 'even though we can't help missing those Calvins. Just a wee bit.'

Dornan was now getting recognised everywhere, not for being an underwear model who appeared on street billboards but as a sadistic murderer. Giggles from girls he met at random were being replaced with shrieks of horror – and Jamie seemed to love it. 'I had one incident in Notting Hill Gate where someone pointed at me and screamed, "There's that serial killer!" That created a bit of a stir. But I love it. I loved playing that sick, sick man … whatever that means.'

Having scared the wits out of four million people on a weekly basis, Jamie was however slightly worried about the repercussions of coming into contact with members of the public. 'I don't get recognised a lot anyway, but I'm slightly anxious about how people will approach me now – because if you see someone being creepy on TV, you automatically assume they're a creepy guy.'

As the last episode, with its cliffhanger ending, was broadcast in June 2013, news had come that a second series was on its way. Dublin actor Emmett Scanlan, who played hard-bitten detective Glen Martin, had made the revelation on Twitter, writing in November 2013: 'Start shooting *The Fall* season two next February. By the sound of it, it's gonna be f*****g awesome. Can't wait.'

While many applauded the BBC's decision, which would see Jamie reprise the role, others were appalled. 'The most repulsive drama ever broadcast on British TV concludes tonight. *The Fall* has featured graphic depictions of sexual murder, violent abuse, necrophilia, stalking, pornography and masturbation,' Christopher Stevens wrote in the *Daily Mail* newspaper. 'BBC executives are defending the show and their decision to renew it for a second series; they claim it provides insight into the motives of a sadistic psychopath [...] The Fall doesn't challenge evil; it wallows in it. This series is an invitation to share an extended rape fantasy.'

'This gratuitously nasty drama was defended by its producer as an attempt to "change the nature of how TV tells crime stories and make them more like real life,"' Allison Pearson wrote in the *Daily Telegraph*. 'Really? When was the last time a serial killer turned out to be a grief counsellor who looks like a male model? Oh and he quoted T.S. Eliot in his killing journal as rapists do.

'If the devil wears Prada 'The Fall' was a snuff movie in a silk blouse.'

Jamie by then hadn't modelled for three years and despite the disapproval from some corners of the press, he was hopeful that playing Spector meant he wouldn't have to return to posing for magazines to earn a crust. 'No matter what I do there will be so many people who won't accept me as an actor because I did modelling. But playing Paul Spector is a start. They can't take that away. It's a role that I hope will alter opinions of me. I've done it and it exists,' he told the *Daily Mirror*. 'I'm proud of the show, really proud of it. But I won't go so far as to say I'm proud of myself.'

Before reprising the role of Spector, though, Jamie admitted that he wanted to do something different, possibly something light-hearted. 'I'd like to play somebody who doesn't murder people for a change. I'd like to do something light. In a perfect world I'd really like to do something funny.'

Fortunately for Jamie, his wish was destiny's command, as his next two roles were a would-be pigeon snatcher and an outlaw with an eighties-style mullet. His friends couldn't help but see the funny side in all that he turned his hand to. No amount of fame would see Jamie's ego inflate – they would see to that. As the Belfast lad jetted to film sets across the world, his pals kept him grounded by sending photos of him as a gawky teenager on WhatsApp. Not that he needed it, of course; Jamie was still as down to earth as they came. 'I would put "ironing shirt sleeves" up there as one of the world's toughest tasks,' he tweeted five days after *The Fall* aired for the first time. He was clearly taking everything in his stride.

Chapter Fourteen

GOING FOR GREY

Jamie was now getting seriously good at auditions. Whereas previously he'd struggled to bag the role, standing nervously in front of casting agents, his experience on *The Fall* had clearly given him newfound confidence.

Soon after filming finished on the Belfast-based crime series, Jamie landed the lead role in Dutch flick *Flying Home*, as director Dominique Deruddere admitted that he was instantly taken with the former Calvin Klein clothes horse.

Jamie was to play Colin, a New York businessman who has to convince the elderly owner of a champion racing pigeon in Belgium to sell his beloved bird to a rich Arab sheik. But Colin ends up falling for his granddaughter. Reading the script was love at first sight for the rising star and having a foreign independent film with an esteemed European director at its helm would undeniably look good on his acting CV. Moreover, playing a man who falls in love with a pretty girl while hunting down a pigeon in Belgium was going to be a walk in the park compared to strangling young women in Belfast, as their eyes bulged in terror. In short, this film ticked all the right boxes. 'I don't read scripts too often that have as much soul as this. I thought the script was really heartfelt, a little bit kooky, a little bit European ... so I ended up doing it because I liked the script and I love Dominique.'

Casting the role hadn't been straightforward. They were looking for someone who fitted the description of 'handsome and successful', which was easy enough, but they also needed someone who could convincingly flit seamlessly between ruthless businessman and sensitive lover. British casting agent Kate Dowd had sent Belgium-born moviemaker Deruddere hundreds of résumés and tapes from young actors keen to scoop the part but no one seemed to have the 'second layer' and depth of character that he was looking for. Until, that is, he stumbled across Jamie. After watching his casting tape, he called up Jamie's agent and asked him in for some tryout sessions. 'He had more to him than his pretty boy look had first revealed,' he said. 'This young fashion model turned out to be a solid actor.

'Further casting sessions with Jamie strengthened my impression that he would be able to act out Colin's deceitful plan without viewers losing sympathy for him.'

'It was very nice working with him,' he added. 'He's a great guy and a very good actor.'

The role was his and Jamie, drawing on all he had learned from

The Fall, quickly got to work on researching the unusual hobby of pigeon fancying – the art and science of breeding pigeons and entering them for races the world over. 'Pigeon fancying is something I knew little about but it's quite an interesting world. There's quite a lot of money to be made from it, which is something I wasn't aware of. The only person I ever knew who'd done it before was boxer Mike Tyson, he is into pigeon fancying in a big way so I guess if someone as high profile as that and as aggressive as that is into something as obscure as pigeon fancying it must be worth something.'

As the summer of 2012 drew to a close, Jamie was enjoying the distinct holiday feeling and little known perks of working on a Flemish movie, as he flitted between the film's locations in Dubai and Belgium. 'Working on a Flemish set is relaxed, everyone is very chilled, obviously there's beer at the end of every day, obviously we still have a lot of work to do but they create a very nice atmosphere,' he said.

The cast was also incredibly welcoming, and Jamie and his on-screen lover Charlotte de Bruyne quickly bonded, particularly since she'd done her homework beforehand by searching for him on the internet in order to garner the inside track into who he was. 'I only knew that he had been a Calvin Klein model. When Googling I really had to chuckle when I read about his relationship with Keira Knightley,' she admitted. 'Jamie was at the beginning of his acting career and so he felt like an equal to me. I felt that he was just as I was, still a little unsure – he may be older but I had the feeling that we were at the same stage in our lives.'

The feeling was mutual and the duo enjoyed some hilarious moments together on set. Whereas Charlotte's English was word-perfect, Jamie amused the cast and crew with his mispronunciation of a variety of Belgian words and, in particular, the director's surname. 'I love Dominique Deruddere, he's brilliant. I was calling him Dominique. What was I saying? Deruuder for a while, thinking that's how you say it but I still can't say it that well. He's amazing; he's like the nicest guy in the world and a great director,' Jamie gushed after filming finished.

Back home, in his swanky pad in London with girlfriend Amelia, it was time to put his feet up before welcoming what would be one of the biggest years of his life, not just professionally but personally. Having just recovered from surgery on his shoulder, and as the year drew to a close, Jamie already had good news to reflect on. The first – and due to the public outcry by *Once Upon A Time* fans after the show's creators killed off his character in the first series – was that Jamie had been invited to go back for a cameo appearance, which he duly accepted.

After returning from his five-week honeymoon in June with Amelia, just as the first episodes of *The Fall* were being screened, it wasn't long before it was back to business and back on set. Jamie had been chosen to star in Channel 4 historical four-part miniseries *New Worlds*, in which he would play an outlaw. Set during the Restoration period, as Charles II took back the throne with a reign of terror, Jamie and his co-stars played young revolutionaries and star-crossed lovers fighting on both sides of the Atlantic. *London Evening Standard* told viewers to 'Expect sex, murder, plotting and treason [...] this will fill a Game of Thrones-shaped hole until the new season starts in April.'

As if that wasn't enough, he had also been nominated for his first-ever acting award and was up for Best Actor for his part in *The Fall* at the forthcoming TV Choice Awards. It was a major feat for someone who just a year before had been a relative unknown in the TV and film world, yet he was now receiving a nomination alongside *Doctor Who*'s Matt Smith and David Tennant in hit ITV drama *Broadchurch*.

Although Jamie didn't make it into the final four for the awards ceremony, he was at least now regarded as being up there with the cream of the industry. And the highly skilled cast on his new show, which included *Skins* actress Freya Mavor and Joe Dempsie from *Games of Thrones*, was testament to how far he'd come. 'It has attracted a diverse and glittering cast,' Channel 4's head of drama Piers Wenger said of the hotly anticipated sequel to 2008 BAFTA-nominated *The Devil's Whore*.

The bloody drama *New Worlds* would see Jamie's character, a rebel named Abe Goffe, trying to overthrow the monarchy in 1680s England. Running around the film with a gun and crossbow was a dream role for Jamie; apart from giving him a respite from the gritty months of playing Paul Spector, it also gave him a chance to play out his boyhood fantasies. 'Being an outlaw was great fun. I'm probably stuck in some transition period from boy to man but I loved all that running through woods with guns, arrows, unwashed hair and your band of mates, indulging my inner Robin Hood.

'Essentially it was the script that drew me then the character that I felt I could play … then I hoped I'd get on with the director and everyone else. On all these counts I have been so lucky with *New Worlds*.'

And like all of his roles – from the ponytailed lover of Kirsten Dunst's Marie Antoinette to love-struck pigeon stalker – there was ample material for Jamie getting a good ribbing. Filming hadn't even started before the laughter broke out on set when the wardrobe team styled Jamie a mullet glued to his own hair, while the rest of the cast sported handsome wigs. Seeing the funny side, he explained: 'It's my real, curly bap – then we added a sort of eighties rock thing around the back and sides to give it that seventeenth century feel. I was happy with it.'

While it was a source of hilarity during its seven-month production in Bristol, with co-stars saying it made him look like a seventeenth-century Russell Brand, it didn't go unnoticed by amused critics either. 'Goffe's wild existence accounts for Dornan's unkempt hair. While most of the cast sport rather elaborate full-head wigs Dornan gets some straggling wisps glued to his own short back and sides,' one noted. Another complained, 'New Worlds Jamie, idealist outlaw Abe, finally appeared after ten minutes but when he did, his mullet was just too distracting.'

Despite the teasing, Jamie had quickly settled into life on set thanks in no small part to his co-stars, in particular Freya who played his on-screen lover Beth. He also enjoyed the heavy historical research behind the character and revelled in learning about a new period of history after the show's writers and creators Martine Brant and Peter Flannery gave them a booklist to work through. 'A couple of books were suggested to us. There was one *Cavalier* by Lucy Worsley that I know Freya and I both read that was recommended by Martine. It became a joke competition between Freya and I to finish it, my copy was more subtly on my iPad but Freya constantly lugged her copy everywhere as I teased and tested her knowledge.

'Because I went to school in Belfast, the English Civil War wasn't high on the curriculum. So to some extent I had to learn from scratch. I had no idea that it was such a barbaric time. We don't want it to be a history lesson but I think audiences will learn something from watching *New Worlds*,' he told the *Sunday Mail*.

As he did with all his characters, Jamie delved deep into their psyche and tried hard to find something within them that he could relate to. In this case, the rising star was convinced that teenagers would be able to identify with the battles his character faced. 'Young people still feel enraged about the same injustices. I like to think people now are treated with greater decency and things aren't as brutal and bloody as they were at that time,' he explained.

Jamie also looked to some of his more boisterous and feisty friends for inspiration when working through how to physicalise the character, since Abe was quick to fight with his hands rather than talking through his concerns. 'The thing about Abe was there's a lot of talk, and he is one of those people who talks with his fists,' Jamie said of the part. 'But you meet these guys, in any time period, who are very headstrong. I have mates like that who are just f**king aggressive. They move a certain way, especially around other people, around new people. They bristle up a little bit. And I tried to draw on some of that for Abe. He isn't comfortable with company outside of his very select few.'

But while it had been an interesting project for Jamie, the reviews were mixed when it premiered the following April. 'Idealists might be inspiring in history books but they don't make for captivating TV characters,' said a review in the *Daily Telegraph*. 'Even Jamie can't save Channel 4's latest historical drama New Worlds. I will probably be thrown in the stocks for saying so but I'll happily take a rotten egg to the face if it means not having to sit through this hammy romp again,' TV critic Oliver Grady added to the complaints. 'His chemistry with leading lady Freya Mavor was convincing but ruined by the writers expecting us to believe her character Beth would have fallen for a man only a few minutes after he abducted her – even if he does look like Jamie Dornan.'

However, perhaps, falling for Dornan's charms in a matter of seconds might not have been wholly unrealistic. Indeed, his next role was to be bigger, better and more extraordinary than the talented man would ever have expected. And a great slice of that Irish charm to which Doran had often attributed his success, rather than to raw talent, would clearly see him right again.

The book on everyone's lips – *Fifty Shades of Grey* – which had sold over 2 million copies in just one month after it hit bookshelves in June 2011 was being made into a film. The steamy novel published by Vintage Books, which made the *New York Times* bestseller list, later became the quickest selling book in history after selling 100 million copies in three years. It revolved around a female college student, Anastasia Steele, who finds herself in a kinky relationship involving sadomasochism and submission with a twenty-seven-year-old billionaire called Christian Grey. The book's two sequels, *Fifty Shades Darker* and *Fifty Shades Freed*, probe into the couple's deepening relationship.

With such a massive readership, largely believed to be women over the age of thirty but also reportedly popular with teenagers and students alike, the erotic must-read was always destined for Hollywood. Its author Erika Leonard, better known under her pen name E.L. James, had orchestrated a deal with careful consideration after countless approaches by film-makers desperate to make it their own. 'I didn't know if [selling it to Hollywood] was the right thing to do. Then I thought, "I'm middle-aged – when in the hell am I going to get another chance to make a movie?"' she admitted.

In March 2012, after a fierce bidding war between ten of the world's top studios, including Sony, Warner Bros and Paramount, James plumped on selling the book's film rights to Universal Pictures and Focus Features in a £3 million deal. The canny British TV executive-turned-author had managed to broker a deal in which she would retain some control during the movie's creative process. As well as hand-picking the director and producers, the forty-eight-year-old mum-of-two revealed that the studios had, in a rare move, also granted her cast and script approvals.

The plucky writer, who admitted a 'midlife crisis' had led to her writing the erotic romance fiction, was won over by

Universal chairman Donna Langley – who 'loved the books' and 'made a great cup of tea' – and Focus president of production Jeb Brody. The latter's previous hits included *Lost in Translation* and *The Pianist*, and she had 'a great background in handling difficult material'. 'I really like clever men who challenge you,' James told *Entertainment Weekly*, 'and with Jeb, I thought, yeah, I can work with that!' After admitting she was given control over most aspects of the film, she added, 'This makes me sound like a control freak, doesn't it.'

The truth was that the kinky antics between powerful businessman Christian and demure student Anastasia were 'every fantasy I'd ever had', the writer claimed, which had been rolled into one steamy and powerfully provocative novel.

Having achieved such unexpected success with the trilogy, the last thing E.L. James wanted was to see the chemistry and sizzling sexual desire between the two main protagonists get lost in translation from page to the big screen. She wanted and needed to ensure that every aspect of their intimate and somewhat debauched relationship was projected flawlessly. 'This is my midlife crisis, all my fantasies out there, it's all in that book. I was a woman obsessed for two years I was writing it everywhere, at home, on the train.

'I'm stunned at how popular it is,' she told America's *Today* programme, adding that she wasn't a 'great writer' and had only penned it as a hobby. Although critics were branding it 'mummy porn', it was a runaway success, translated into fifty-one different languages and winning rave reviews from fans around the world. 'It makes you squirm in your seat,' a businesswoman in her twenties admitted to a TV show. 'Women who are reading it say they are having more sex with their husbands,' a therapist revealed, while a mother-of-three told one of the hundreds of internet forums that had sprung up about the book, 'it definitely, for lack of a better word, gets you going.'

It was evidently hugely important to James to 'get it right'. 'This is huge. There is this passionate fandom, we need to get this right for them,' she explained. Moreover, *Fifty Shades of Grey* was also quickly becoming a multimillion-pound brand which would bring with it a range of spin-off merchandise, including a CD of music the author wrote the story to, bottles of wine, T-shirts with slogans from the book and sex toys such as the infamous silver pleasure balls, handcuffs and crops, as immortalised in the series.

News of the forthcoming *Fifty Shades* movie, meanwhile, had spread like wildfire across Hollywood, sparking a feeding frenzy within all areas of production. Top producers such as Brian Grazer, Adam Shankman, Scott Stuber, Doug and Lucy Wick, and Stacy Cramer had all reportedly been courting James and her agent Valerie Hoskins. It was important that E.L. James had the perfect team and, along with the bigwigs at Universal and Focus, she decided to hire Michael De Luca and Dana Brunetti, producers of *The Social Network* for which they won a Best Picture Oscar nomination. 'At its core, *Fifty Shades of Grey* is a complex love story, requiring a delicate and sophisticated hand to bring it to the big screen,' said Universal co-chairman Donna Langley in a statement. 'Mike and Dana's credits more than exemplify what we need in creative partners, and we're glad to have them as part of our team.' Both producers had been known for their work on book adaptations. As well as their collaboration with producer Scott Rudin on the 2010 drama *The Social Network* – based on the creators of Facebook and adapted from the non-fiction book *The Accidental Billionaires* – De Luca had also produced 2011 hit baseball movie *Moneyball*, based on the book *Moneyball: The Art of Winning*.

The next job was to hire a director along with a stellar cast, most importantly securing the right Christian Grey. Finding someone able to fill the criteria needed was going to be tough, chiefly because every reader – all 100 million of them – had created in their mind a very exact image of what the sadistic, controlling billionaire looked like. Few casting agents could have experienced that kind of pressure before.

The first description of the powerful businessman in the novel said it all: 'This Christian Grey is the richest, most elusive, most enigmatic bachelor in Washington State.' As if that wasn't a big enough ask, the right man for the job would also have to plausibly fit the description: 'the epitome of male beauty, breathtaking.' The domineering heart-throb was exactly what all women secretly wanted, as the author claimed, and the actor would have to be able to convincingly fulfill that fantasy. 'I think in their fantasies that's what women desire, in real life it's something very different, it's probably someone who can do the dishes. [He is rich and domineering] because that's really attractive on paper. You're in charge of your job, you're in charge of your house, your children, getting them food on the table, you're doing this all of the time and it would be nice for someone else to just be in charge for a bit,' she explained to America's *Today* programme.

Film agents were desperately looking through their books, trying to find the winning actor they could put forward for this most coveted of roles and amongst them was Jamie Dornan. Still feeling like 'the skinny boy at school', he never expected to land the job – that would, of course, have been too good to be true – but his casting tape was duly sent in.

They hype surrounding the film was still raging and in June 2013 a director was announced. Sam Taylor-Johnson, a British mother-of-four best known for the movie *Nowhere Boy* – a biopic about the Beatles star John Lennon – had beaten off stiff competition for the role, which purportedly included Hollywood beauty Angelina Jolie. Honoured to have been chosen by E.L. James, Sam vowed, as a *Fifty Shades* fan, to do it justice. 'I am excited to be charged with the evolution of *Fifty Shades Of Grey* from page to screen,' she said in a press statement in June 2013. 'For the legions of fans, I want to say that I will honour the power of Erika's book and the characters of Christian and Anastasia. They are under my skin too.'

Whether Jamie would be Sam's Christian still remained to be seen but two weeks after her appointment, the actor had his own life-changing announcement to make. He had landed the role of his dreams. Two weeks after his picture-perfect wedding to beautiful Amelia, it was time to tell the world: Jamie Dornan was going to be a father.

Chapter Fifteen

A BIG ANNOUNCEMENT

Jamie couldn't hide his excitement; he was going to see his baby for the very first time. Standing in his obstetrician dad's private clinic back home in Belfast with beautiful Amelia by his side – already blossoming with a small baby bump – they were ready for the scan. In true Dornan family style, this was a moment no one wanted to miss so it wasn't just Jamie and Amelia in the room, waiting to catch the first glimpse of the latest addition to the close-knit clan. Jamie's step-mum Samina, now a qualified and well-respected obstetrician in her own right, had agreed to perform the scan herself. Amelia couldn't have been in better hands; caring Samina, now a consultant in maternal fetal medicine in the city's Royal Maternity Hospital, was used to carrying them out on pregnant women daily. And seeing her third grandchild wiggling about on the screen was a proud and magical experience. 'The early wellbeing scanning was a beautiful and emotional experience for all present,' she told local newspaper *Sunday Life* soon after. 'Jim and I are delighted that our third grandchild is on the way.'

It had indeed been a poignant moment for everyone inside the room. Fifteen years after Jamie's mum Lorna had died from cancer and with his dad Jim now living daily with leukaemia, getting to the happy point of becoming a parent himself had seen Jamie endure some incredibly tough times. But this was all he had ever wanted. All those who knew and loved Jamie were aware that he had hoped to become a father for many years, as he once admitted that he was broody 'just seeing strangers' babies'.

Peering in on the tiny newborns, while he followed his dad around on Saturday morning ward rounds as an inquisitive schoolboy, had also clearly stuck with him. As an adult, his deep interest in his 'baby doctor' father's life-changing job remained and just before announcing his impending fatherhood, Jamie became patron of premature baby charity Tinylife, of which his dad Jim was president.

With all those paternal instincts firmly in place and after having seen his baby alive and well on its first scan, the star was ready to embrace all that came with being a new parent – including the crying, changing dirty nappies and the dreaded sleep deprivation. It was clear that Jamie was going to approach his role of being a father with as much gusto and positivity as he would any acting role. 'You might sleep a bit less but you've got this small life to look after,' Jamie said of parents who moan about being tired with a newborn. 'I am quite good on little sleep. I think a lot of that is an attitude thing. I think the same about hangovers. You can compound your misery by not getting out of bed and not facing the day. But if you actually get the f*** up you might not be as miserable,' he added in an interview to the *Daily Telegraph* newspaper.

Married life was going well for the loved-up duo; while remaining tight-lipped to the public about his baby, Jamie did admit to enjoying his honeymoon period with Amelia, two months after their nuptials. 'It's going well so far. It's only been seven weeks and so it's all fairly fresh,' he said of his marriage. 'It doesn't feel massively different to how our life was before. It's good fun.'

Preparations for the pitter-patter of tiny feet were also in full swing. Where to have the baby was one consideration and although it would have made sense for Jamie's dad, as an expert in the field, to deliver his grandchild, Jim later admitted that it was never the plan. 'I wasn't in the delivery room for my grandchildren, I wasn't even in the delivery room for my first child, even though I was an obstetrician I was told to leave the room in those days. I'm not sure it's a particularly good idea,' he admitted. Whatever was going to happen on the day, this new life was going to be loved and cherished, and would undeniably benefit from the Dornan family's down-to-earth nature and love of life. And whichever way his career was going to turn in the next six months, Jamie's father was going to be proudly watching this latest development in his son's life with interest, while enjoying all the perks of being a grandfather. 'I actually found the whole thing [of becoming a grandfather] seamless, I feel like my grandchildren are actually my children. I have such a love for babies and everything that goes with them. There's no doubt that the best thing about grandchildren is that you can hand them back,' he admitted.

However, for notoriously private Jamie becoming a parent in the public eye would throw up more hazards than most new fathers would have to deal with. As well as the general worries that come with dealing with a fragile newborn, the actor – who was on the cusp of becoming one of the most famous stars of his generation – was facing having to fight tooth and nail to protect the privacy of his new family. Even before announcing Amelia's pregnancy, photos of the pair eating in a restaurant had emerged in the press, questioning if fatherhood was on the cards, since his wife was drinking water at the table. In the coming months, additional glossy snaps, snatched from the roadside, appeared in more newspapers and magazine, as the actor and mother-to-be went about their daily business, shopping, chatting and going out for a coffee. With an already well-entrenched hate of the paparazzi and ongoing disbelief at the ridiculous rumours that crop up in the gossip press, Jamie was about to enter unknown territory as Celebrity Dad.

For the moment, though, that seemed a world away, since superstardom at the time appeared highly improbable. Jamie had been waiting to hear if his audition tape for *Fifty Shades of Grey* had been good enough to get a callback. Much to his disappointment, it hadn't – someone else had landed the part of Christian Grey.

Chapter Sixteen

BAGGING THE LEAD

'I am delighted to let you know that the lovely Dakota Johnson has agreed to be our Anastasia in the film adaptation of Fifty Shades of Grey,' E.L. James tweeted to her fans on 3 September 2013. This announcement was followed two minutes later by: 'The gorgeous and talented Charlie Hunnam will be Christian Grey.'

The punishingly long wait was over. After months of speculation over which Hollywood stars would be picked to play the sizzling leads, two relative unknowns had been chosen. *Sons of Anarchy* star Charlie, a British actor whose earliest starring role was in kids' TV drama *Byker Grove*, had landed the part of ice-cold, sadomasochistic businessman Christian. It had been an 'awesome audition' according to producers and the chemistry between the blond hunk and twenty-three-year-old Californian Dakota, as his willing sex slave Ana, was reportedly so potent that when asked to act out a bedroom scene, the part was his.

Jamie was undeniably disappointed. And, truth be told, he wasn't the only one. While the *Fifty Shades* team, along with the author, were 'thrilled' with their decision, tens of thousands of fans were outraged. They had been whipped into a frenzy following weeks of whispers in the press and online gossip forums over who was likely to land the much-coveted roles. Many mentioned were A-listers, with *Twilight* heart-throb Robert Pattinson – said to be E.L. James's top choice – at the forefront. On the other hand, the studio had reportedly offered *The Notebook* star Ryan Gosling – a favourite with the book's readers who had dedicated whole fan pages to him filling the alluring role – the part. Other actors tipped to have been in the mix included Matt Bomer, Alexander Skarsgard, Theo James and Christian Cooke.

The shortlist for pretty college student Anastasia, meanwhile, was made up of six possible actors – all relatively unknown – including Imogen Poots, who had starred in *Jane Eyre* and American Elizabeth Olsen, who was nominated for the BAFTA Rising Star Award earlier in the year. However, stunning Dakota, the daughter of *Miami Vice* star Don Johnson and Melanie Griffith, had impressed in the audition room beyond expectation. 'She looks too old,' one fan moaned on a forum. 'I'm not sure she can pull off sexy but I suppose we'll have to wait and see what she can pull out of the bag,' another said.

Her future co-star Hunnam, though, was confident that they could pull it off and tried to allay fans' concerns. 'I felt really intrigued and excited about the role of Christian so I went and read the first book to get a clearer idea of who this character was, and I felt even more excited at the prospect of bringing him to life,' he said of the audition process. 'We [Taylor-Johnson and I] kind of both suggested I do a reading with Dakota, who was her favourite, and as soon as we got in the room and I started reading with Dakota I knew that I definitely wanted to do it. There's just like a tangible chemistry between us. It felt exciting and fun and weird and compelling.'

By all accounts, the two actors – suddenly thrust into the world's spotlight with the announcement – were overwhelmed and excited to be 'entrusted with the roles' in such a high-profile movie. Overnight, Geordie actor Charlie's life was turned upside down. Not only were interview requests coming in ten to the dozen, neighbours reported that fans of the book were leaving their lacy underwear draped over the doorknob to his house. 'We've seen frilly knickers, bras and even stockings left at his door by women as they try to get his attention. It's very odd, we've never seen anything like it,' one neighbour told a newspaper.

As if that wasn't stressful enough, much to Hunnam's horror, an internet campaign was launched against him and Dakota playing Christian and Anastasia. An ensuing online petition of over 80,000 names demanding that Universal Studios axe the pair, immediately made world news, as fans threatened to boycott the film on its release. In a US poll, 54 per cent voted to have new faces hired for the two kinky roles and as the weeks progressed, there seemed to be no let-up in the public outcry. One disgusted fan wrote, 'Christian is supposed to be sexy and mysterious. Charlie Hunnam looks dirty and very unappealing. I will not be watching the film with this cast.'

The much-anticipated launch of *Fifty Shades* was quickly descending into chaos, with social networking site Twitter awash with hateful comments towards the male actor, alongside complaints that he had been grossly miscast. Although just as many had leapt to Hunnam's defence, saying that while he may not have the right 'look', he certainly had the required charm and charisma, it was too late. One month after accepting the role, the star quit. Even though he cited a busy TV schedule for leaving, explaining he wouldn't have enough time to prepare for the role of Christian, insiders claimed that the star had got cold feet after being 'overwhelmed' by the public attention. He also reportedly had creative differences with the *Fifty Shades* team, including demanding script changes. As studio bosses were forced to hire a pair of bulky bodyguards to protect the stunned actor from crazed fans, others believed he simply couldn't cope with the negative backlash. The actor later confessed that it was a combination of factors, admitting he had been close to a breakdown.

With filming in Canada scheduled to start in three weeks, there was no time to lose: Sam Taylor-Johnson and the team had to go back to the drawing board to find their perfect Christian. Back home in London, Jamie Dornan had heard the news and was wondering whether he may be given a second chance. 'When Charlie dropped out I didn't instantly think "Oh here we go, maybe I should cancel the holiday," but I did feel that maybe we'd revisit the idea of me,' he admitted.

The assumption was right; his tape had finally caught the eye of casting chiefs and he was invited for a last-minute face-to-face audition. Erika was already backing his corner. As a big fan of *The Fall*, she believed that his detached way of delivering Spector in the thrilling crime series was exactly the measured and controlled manner she was looking for in the actor playing Christian. It was true to say that Paul Spector's chilling killer instinct was not dissimilar from megalomaniac Grey's penchant for stalking and S&M, and if Jamie could nail that kind of tone again, he was in with a fighting chance.

Five days after Charlie had publicly quit, Dornan was on a flight to Los Angeles for an intense one-day tryout with Dakota Johnson. With producers desperate to fill the role, Jamie was plunged right into the action in front of the tough panel which included Erika and director Sam Taylor-Johnson. After meeting Dakota, they were told to re-enact two of the most crucial scenes in the book: the interview when Ana first meets Christian in his spacious office in Seattle, followed by the 'climatic scene' near the end of the book, which would inevitably include Jamie interacting sexually with the actress for the first time. Ensuring there was powerful chemistry between them was imperative. 'There's quite a lot going on in both scenes,' Jamie said of the all-important audition. 'The interview scene is sort of a condensed version of the journey that the two of them go on. There are so many layers in it. It's a beast.'

While the book puts the reader inside Ana's head, so we know what she's thinking, Christian was going to be much harder to read and much of their sexually charged and emotional moments within the story would likely be filling that communication gap.

Thankfully for Jamie, he managed to pull it off beautifully. As they acted out the 'climatic scene', the sexual desire between the muscular ex-model and his quirky co-star was both satisfyingly convincing and mesmerising. It was exactly what Erika had been hoping for. Not only did Jamie and Dakota work together in the attractiveness stakes, but there was a genuine ease between the pair of them, which would make it easier for them as actors to work through some of the more sexually explicit scenes. Communication and camaraderie were as important as chemistry, and the twosome clearly had them in buckets. 'I presumed we had chemistry right away because they made it happen with us,' Jamie said. 'That's a big part of it, having that [chemistry] and having trust because we got ourselves into situations that don't feel natural and aren't that easy and you definitely need to have that trust there.'

Moreover, Jamie looked spectacular on camera, as one would expect from a millionaire model. Ultimately, he could justly fit the description of twenty-seven-year-old Christian.

A journalist had written of Jamie prior to an interview, 'The actor miraculously packs away the good looks – lapis lazuli eyes, delicate bones, he even has pretty ears.' Thankfully, Jamie was more straightforward in personality than his screen alter ego. 'He has nothing of the unhinged about him, no flicker of menace, only the genuine charm of someone who is never trying to charm,' he continued.

It was very clear that they had found their man – and, even

better for Jamie, his modelling past wasn't going to put him on a back foot. As fictional Christian is described in the romantic novel as one of the best-looking men in the world and Jamie had once been dubbed 'the male Kate Moss', this project was his best chance of getting his foot firmly on the rung of that Hollywood ladder.

It was the perfect role. 'Modelling doesn't hold you back in LA at all,' he explained. 'In LA they don't think that because you leant against walls and looked depressed while someone took your photograph, it means you can't act. In the UK there's a massive stigma to it. You couldn't possibly have had your photograph taken for a living and act.'

What clinched it was the fact that the producers were sold on the idea that Christian and Ana shouldn't be played by already established Hollywood stars – instead, these roles should launch them higher into the echelons of Tinseltown royalty. 'I always thought it would be better if we went with somebody unknown so everyone can discover them together, that's where I really think we are now with Jamie and Dakota,' Dana Brunetti admitted some months later.

It was by all accounts, one of Jamie's more successful auditions and he returned home to London, to his pregnant wife Amelia, to wait for the call, which came just a few days later at two o'clock in the morning. Knowing that the decision was coming at such an unsociable hour, with Los Angeles eight hours behind, Jamie had stayed up especially in his pyjamas. When the phone finally rang, he was sitting on his sofa, clutching the handset nervously and watching reruns of *Storage Wars* on TV to try to stay calm.

'I was sort of pretending I wasn't waiting, but the phone was in my hand, halfway to my ear,' he said.

It was Sam Taylor-Johnson on the line – and this time he heard the news he was hoping for: Christian Grey was his for the taking. That's if he wanted it. There had, of course, been one very important consideration to make in accepting the role: his first child was due around the exact time when shooting was due to start, at the beginning of November. Ultimately, Jamie wanted his wife Amelia's blessing before taking on the biggest role in his life to date. He also wanted to ensure that he would be there for the most important day in his life, seeing his first child being born.

For Amelia, her husband playing Christian meant facing the prospect of flying with him to Vancouver, heavily pregnant and hundreds of miles from home, where she would give birth in a hospital close to the movie set. 'Amelia is in her last trimester of pregnancy. She was Jamie's main concern when it came to signing the contract because he would be away from her for a large chunk of time while filming,' a friend admitted at the time. After extensive talks, the pair decided that Jamie should go for it. 'They've agreed it is too good an opportunity for him to turn down,' the source added.

Jamie told Sam that the answer was 'yes'. He was to play Christian Grey and thus become the object of millions of women's fantasies. Even though it was a huge milestone in the thirty-one-year-old star's career – a turning point – there was no champagne on ice after accepting the role. In fact his reaction couldn't have been further from how his screen alter ego would have greeted such news. 'It was pretty exciting getting that call, I was in London at the time, it was 2 am and I was kind of waiting for it. But I was asleep pretty soon after I found out,' he admitted to the *Today* programme. 'You know I wasn't in a normal time zone where I could go out and party and stuff. My heavily pregnant wife was downstairs sleeping so I just went downstairs and joined her in bed and went to sleep!'

A week after the audition, E.L. James announced the news on her Twitter feed. 'Stow your twitchy palms ladies … our man is here.'

'Welcome to TeamFifty@JamieDornan1 x'

When asked how she felt about the new choice, she added: 'Thrilled'. Fans who had campaigned to get rid of Hunnam seemed ecstatic at the casting and flooded online blogs and forums to signal their approval. Crissy Maier, co-founder of the *Fifty Shades* fan site *Laters, Baby*, said, 'He has the right look and he's also new enough that he probably doesn't have a high price tag … I like his underwear ads myself.'

In fact, Jamie had driven quite a hard bargain before accepting the part, convincing producers to agree to a series of demands alongside a base salary of £80,000 for the first movie. As *The Sun* pointed out, 'If Jamie Dornan is as ruthless at wielding a whip as he is in business negotiations he's going to leave his *Fifty Shades of Grey* co-star very sore indeed.' The biggest coup in the deal was sealing a share of the film's profits, which will see him a very rich man if the much-hyped movie proves to be a box office triumph. His agent also wangled him a guarantee that he could leave the set when Amelia went into labour, thus enabling him to spend some time with his wife and newborn. On top of that, with a new series of *The Fall* due to start shooting in the early part of 2014, he insisted that all his scenes were wrapped up in time for him to honour that commitment. 'Jamie has played this to his advantage amazingly – he's very savvy about the deal he's netted. A share in the movie's profits will bring stacks of cash,' a source told *The Sun* newspaper at the time.

With news that E.L. James had sold the film rights for all three books in the trilogy, Jamie had also secured plenty of work and cash for the future – perfect for a man about to start a family of his own. And although not everyone was satisfied with Jamie playing Christian, public feeling had been nothing like the reaction that Hunnam had provoked. 'He was horribly attractive in *The Fall*,' said Jane Crowther, editor of *Total Film*. 'He demonstrated real darkness; he was really creepy. Terrifying, actually. That push-pull of attraction and revulsion is interesting. I hope he'll bring that darkness to *Fifty Shades*, so it's not just a silly, sexy romp.'

Author E.L. James was also getting incredible feedback from fans who were complimenting her on choosing the former Dior model. 'Good choice my lady!!! You did good :)' one wrote. 'OH. MY. GOOOD! Great news! He's perfect for the role! We. Love. You!!!' another gushed.

The cream of Hollywood was also backing her choice, with stars praising the author on Twitter. 'I'm a monstrous Jamie fan. Wasn't allowed to be attracted to him on The Fall because he played a sex murderer. 50 Shades is my big chance!' wrote actress Lena Dunham. 'Congrats to the sweetest person/scariest actor

I know! 50 Shades of Grey just got real. So f***n psyched,' said Hollywood star Kate Mara, while esteemed writer Bret Easton Ellis wrote: 'I think that Jamie Dornan is the perfect choice to play Christian Grey. Smartest casting decision in a long time.' Even his ex Keira Knightley agreed that he was the perfect choice to play the sexy fiend. When asked about her former lover's raunchy part, she bashfully admitted, 'He's very good looking, all the girls will love him.'

Erika was over the moon with her casting. 'There was a huge online reaction when Charlie Hunnam was initially cast as Christian. It was very mixed and I had to get off Twitter. And then he dropped out. It was disappointing, but it is what it is. Now we have Jamie, and that's great. It's been interesting with Jamie, the fan reaction has been so positive.'

Jamie's family were also thrilled with the news and celebrated with a Sunday roast at his house in West London. Hardly the lavish celebration one would expect from a now legitimate Hollywood actor, but it was again testament to his down-to-earth attitude and long-held tradition that family came first. His father Jim was justly proud and, having read *Fifty Shades of Grey* himself, was the biggest supporter when his son decided to go for the role. Unlike Dakota, who admitted she wouldn't want her parents to watch her in the sexually explicit film, Jamie said that his 'liberal' family wouldn't be shocked by his on-screen goings-on. 'I'm a fairly worldly guy. I grew up in a very liberal place. I'm not saying we had a playroom, but I'm not shocked by [the sex in the book]. It's essential to tell the story. I can't believe films that don't invoke the sexual side of it. So it works for me,' he said. 'My dad was all for it. I don't come from a cagey family,' he added to *GQ* magazine.

Jim himself commented to the *Daily Mail* newspaper, 'Jamie might be playing Christian Grey, but he has inherited a total respect and commitment to women and women's rights. We are all that way in the family. Jamie and my two daughters are very pro-women – I have influenced them with that. As with the role Jamie's playing, a lot of people are into all sorts of things, and I don't think we should knock anything that people consent to.' His two sisters were also incredibly proud of their younger brother and his father Jim confirmed that despite his newfound super fame, they were as close as ever. 'They are very protective of him but it's almost the other way round, he is of them, he's a great brother, we are a very tight family and they all look to each other and I think when they lost their mum it does bring them very closely together. That bond will be there forever and they love him and are very proud of him,' he told a Seattle radio show.

With so much expectation heaped on him, from fans to film producers alike, one would have expected Jamie to be nervous about playing the sadistic billionaire. After all, spending almost an entire film half-naked, sometimes with bondage whip in hand, would fill many with terror – not so Jamie Dornan. A few weeks before filming was due to start, he seemed unflappable. 'I certainly don't fear it,' he said. 'I already got a glimpse into working with the director Sam at the test, and I'd met Dakota by then. So I had a glimpse into how I felt it would be if I got the part. None of it scared me,' he admitted.

The movie, after all, wasn't going to be a porn film, and Jamie had years of experience stripping naked for the camera. It was second nature to him. Having read the script, he was also keen to point out that it wasn't going to be as raunchy and X-rated as the book. 'In some ways, it'll break some boundaries. But at the same time they want to put bums on seats. They can't alienate an audience. It's got to be watchable,' he explained. 'It can't be hardcore. I wouldn't have signed up to it if it was. You've got to make something a large amount of people can go and see. It's not going to be grotesque.'

With that in mind, his main aim was to try to please as many of the book readers as possible, as the ultimate challenge was not being hated by the public when the film was finally released. 'I just want to please a decent percentage of people who read the book because people hold the book so close to their hearts, so, you know, I'm not going to please everyone but I hope I've done a good enough job and I'm not totally hated at the end of it,' he added.

Jamie's main challenge at the time, however, was learning his lines. With a film start date set for the beginning of November and having landed the lead role less than a month before, it was near on impossible. Filming in Vancouver was pushed back to December, along with a rescheduled release date from August to 13 February 2015 – in time for Valentine's Day weekend. Movie insiders claimed that the move was less about production and more about Universal Pictures wanting to maximise on branding and box office sales by tying in with Valentine's Day. 'They will be hoping '50 Shades' becomes a Valentine's weekend "date film" or for those that are single, it will provide an opportunity to go out on that day and indulge in a little bit of kinkiness. The merchandise they could sell around this time would also be incredibly profitable. Rescheduling was a very wise move,' an insider revealed.

The studio was even worried that their original August date would be hampered by women going on family holidays abroad. It released in a statement: 'We see this movie as a global event. The strength of this book is really worldwide, so we want to be able to take advantage of women who are invariably on vacation with their families during the month of August in Europe.'

With a release confirmed a day shy of Valentine's Day, a first peek of Jamie and Dakota together, as Christian and Anastasia, appeared on the front of American glossy showbiz magazine *Entertainment Weekly* two weeks before filming started. The former Dior model posed in a grey suit with a protective arm around his brunette co-star while a silver-grey tie hanged whip-like from a protective hand cupping her shoulder. It was a powerful image – and the public seemed impressed. 'The perfect Christian. Jamie Dornan is sizzling!' one critic wrote. 'Mmm, Mr Dornan will see you now!' a fan gushed on a *Fifty Shades* fan site. 'I literally can't wait for the film to come out now, roll on February 14th 2015, I will be there in the front row Jamie.'

Much to the public's delight, there was more good news in store for Jamie fans. Movie bosses were toying with the idea of releasing an explicit version of the film, as well as its fifteen-rated release, where the model would be seen romping in X-rated scenes as 'dirty' as the kinky book. Producer Dana Brunetti said,

'Everybody could go and enjoy the 15s version, and then if they really wanted to see it again and get a little bit more gritty with it then have that 18s version out there as well. It'd be great for the studio too because they'd get a double dip on the box office. What we're kind of hearing from the fans is they want it dirty.

'They want it as close as possible to the book. We want to keep it elevated but also give the fans what they want.'

However, closer to the film's release there were plans to give it an eighteen certificate, with a possible unrated cut on DVD. 'Well, there is going to be a lot of sex in the film,' screenwriter Kelly Marcel explained. 'It will be NC-17 [the equivalent of a British 18 certificate]. It's going to be raunchy. We are 100 per cent going there ... We did go through and decide which are our favourite moments and which are not. Most of them are in there, but I can't say more than that.'

Jamie added to the excitement by admitting that he was champing at the bit to get stuck into the sex scenes, explaining that it was 'essential to tell the story'. Producer Dana was delighted that the thirty-one-year-old was so keen to get cracking on the sadistic scenes. 'You have to get actors that really want to do it as well, and that was a really difficult process. A lot of them didn't want to do it just because of what they either thought that it would require or what it will require, or what it will make them into. It's gonna make them into huge stars,' she said.

The film had now been cast and Jamie was in good company. Fellow cast members included US actor Victor Rasuk as the aspiring photographer Jose Rodriguez, who is also Christian's love rival, and *True Blood* star Luke Grimes as Christian's younger brother, Elliot. British singer Rita Ora had landed the role of Christian's adopted younger sister Mia, while American TV beauty Eloise Mumford was starring as Anastasia's roommate and best friend Kate Kavanagh.

Jamie only had a few weeks to prepare for the part before leaving for Vancouver. As well as starting the arduous task of learning lines, Jamie was training in the gym to ensure that Christian had the rippling abs and strong, powerful thighs that his female fans would be looking for. 'I've never felt that Christian needs to be some kind of monster, but I think it's very clear how he conditions himself and looks after himself,' he told *Entertainment Weekly*. 'I take decent enough care of myself anyway, so obviously I'm gonna up it slightly with training, but we don't have any intention to really bulk up. I don't think it's appropriate.'

His co-star Dakota had joined him in a gym routine, desperate not to be shown up by Jamie's enviable muscular physique in their countless nude scenes together. 'Obviously, I want to look good naked,' she said. 'I totally understand now why people exercise because it kind of f****** feels awesome.'

As someone who had spent most of his working life in a pair of freshly pressed underpants, Jamie now had to get used to wearing a suit. Although his character lived in immaculately tailored outfits twenty-four/seven, the model-turned-actor clearly tended to pull them from the back of his wardrobe for special occasions. Jamie's closet of jeans, jumpers and old shirts seemed as far removed from his alter ego's as he could get. 'My one staple in my wardrobe is this old blue shirt that I bought in J Crew about five years ago, I think it's got stains under the armpits, I still go for that most days,' he admitted. Not so for the movie role of the year; Jamie was being measured up by the wardrobe department headed by Oscar-winning costume designer Mark Bridges for a collection of fine designer grey suits. While he couldn't prepare for it beforehand, by the end of the three-month film shoot, being well turned out in a snappy suit was something that had started to feel second nature. And the fashion industry had started to speculate if top designers had been allowed to dress Jamie Dornan in his iconic role. 'With major fashion labels like Armani and Prada playing a role in recent movies, I have to wonder whether the *Fifty Shades* wardrobe will serve as a form of product placement? I wonder if the execs at Calvin Klein are clamouring to get Christian Grey into a pair of their tighty whities,' one journalist mused.

However, for Jamie the actor, stepping into one of Christian's suits was not only a way of portraying the image, it was also key in getting into the role … adopting his 'look' was essential for getting into the character's headspace too – as was preparing for his raunchy sex scenes, which he did by watching box sets of *Sex in the City*. While still filming *New Worlds*, Jamie, along with his co-star Joe Dempsie, carried out some research by watching the US sitcom which starred Sarah Jessica Parker as Carrie. 'Joe and I watched all the *Sex And The City* box sets – twice. That helped,' he admitted.

Jamie and director Sam Taylor-Johnson had also started to map the complicated character out together. 'I think there was so much to Christian that we covered. Someone who is careful to keep himself in shape, someone who spends obscene amounts of money on presenting himself [...].

A lot of that work was done in the gym and with costume. We didn't talk about particulars of the way he would move but I'm quite awkward in a suit because I don't have an opportunity to wear a suit very often, and this is a guy who lives in a suit – the best suit. That has to have an effect. But when you end up in a suit for 80 per cent of the filming process, you become pretty comfortable with it.'

Preparing for the role also included performing a complete character assassination of the sadomasochistic businessman: who was this alluring Christian Grey? Where did his knowledge and lust for bondage come from and why does he get off completely controlling virgin Anastasia's life? For Jamie it was important to try to understand where his motivation came from. Building up a picture of Christian's dark past was relatively easy. He was neglected by his prostitute mother as a child, physically abused by her pimp who beat him up and used him as an ashtray as a young boy, and as a teenager was sexually abused and 'dominated' by a friend of his adopted mother. The key for Jamie was identifying that Christian was a 'broken' person. 'I see broken people as those who have been through hardship – whether it's really ugly hardship like abandonment, abuse, something definitively life altering, like Christian Grey,' he told *Interview* magazine. 'There are reasons for these people being the way they are, and that's what drives them.'

As for his part of counsellor-turned-killer in *The Fall*, Jamie was also keen to try to find something within Christian that he liked, believing that the more he could lose himself in the role, the more believable that character would become to his audience. 'I'm not like Christian but I understand him perfectly,' he told *Glamour* magazine. 'I never thought he was a monster. He is simply woven from his desires as every one of us are.

'I want to keep an element of myself in every character I play. And maybe that's connected to finding something that you like in every character,' he explained further.

On studying Christian, and despite his very dark side, Jamie wouldn't have been short of qualities to admire. Not only is the 'difficult' character a one-woman man who is clearly in love with Anastasia, the entrepreneur was also a philanthropist who liked to give to the needy, sought counselling for his issues and was modest about his attractiveness. '[The characters I've played do have two sides]. Even Christian has two sides,' he said. 'Come to think of it, he has fifty!'

With lines learnt and preparation underway, Jamie was finally ready to take on the challenge of embodying Christian Grey on set in Vancouver. The paparazzi were hot on his heels and in the weeks running up to the start of filming, snaps of Jamie and his heavily pregnant wife Amelia trying to enjoy their last childless days together began cropping up in the press. Drinking coffee, laughing as they strolled down the street, holding hands … even the most mundane of tasks were being lapped up by the photographers and splashed across the press. Ten years since his very public relationship with Keira Knightley, he had become overnight tabloid fodder once again – except this time he was the one the Fleet Street editors were chasing. However, ten years wiser, protective Jamie was determined not to let it affect him and his much-loved family. 'There are so many ways to make a living that don't involve hiding in bushes opposite a house with a camera in your hand, that's not making a living that's making a choice to be a perverted f***head,' Jamie said of the intrusion of the paparazzi in the wake of his *Fifty Shades* role.

For the time being Jamie wasn't unnerved by the attention. 'It doesn't feel mental on the inside,' he said of his overnight fame. 'I'm sure from the outside it looks crazy, but I'm lucky I'm on the inside.' It was indeed fortunate that Jamie had become such a seasoned expert at keeping a cool head because at that time, more than ever, he would need it. Not on the film set, mind you, but in the delivery room. Not long after filming started in Vancouver, the news was confirmed: Jamie Dornan had a daughter.

Chapter Seventeen

THE DADDY OF
ALL ROLES

Everything was happening at once. Not only was Jamie starting the biggest role of his career, he was knee-deep in nappies. His real-life leading lady Amelia had given birth to a beautiful baby girl and the actor was smitten. Surrounded by their adoring family, the actor and his wife were overjoyed at becoming new parents and were quickly finding their feet, away from the public eye.

Jamie was relishing being a father and not even the sleepless nights which are part and parcel of life with a newborn lessened his enjoyment of being a parent. With his days of drinking long gone, a night in with Amelia watching TV with their daughter happy sleeping upstairs was bliss. 'I don't understand people complaining about babies. Sure, I miss a bit of sleep, but look at the rewards – better than not being able to sleep because of a hangover,' the new dad confided.

Jamie's proud father Jim was also thrilled with being a grandfather again and was impressed with how well his son was handling his new life-changing job. He said of Jamie after the birth of his baby girl, 'It's wonderful watching them interacting and seeing them go on the same learning curves as we did; how to deal with them, how to soothe them, how to cope with all their problems and you do have to watch that you don't just give constant advice but it's tempting. It's interesting that people like to have a little bit of your life but Jamie's a very private man understandably so yeah, I think, we enjoy people thinking he's done a good job.'

As the world's media had kept its eyes focused on every morsel of gossip from the *Fifty Shades of Grey* set, it was amazing that Jamie's stunning and heavily pregnant wife had managed to go into labour, deliver a baby and enjoy a few precious weeks with her famous husband as a new unit before the press caught wind of it. Indeed, it wasn't until two weeks after the start of filming in Vancouver on a chilly, autumnal film set that the news of his baby finally broke. 'Jamie and Amelia Dornan are delighted to announce the birth of their baby daughter born at the end of November,' his agent said in a statement to the press on 16 December. Jamie had carried out the first task as protective dad perfectly.

His next challenge was working out how to juggle his fatherly duties while taking on the biggest challenge in his acting career to date. Taking inspiration from his doctor father all those years before, who had allowed Jamie to follow him around the hospital on weekend ward rounds, Jamie let his wife and baby daughter come to his work too. While Amelia and their newborn weren't permanent fixtures on the film set by any means, they would visit Jamie as often as they could and were quickly welcomed into the *Fifty Shades* family. He had also rented a comfortable family home, complete with Christmas tree, in Vancouver so that they could spend the holiday season together. Although Jamie wouldn't be enjoying a turkey dinner and present-opening session with his family back in Belfast for the first time in his life, it was at least a chance to make his daughter's first Christmas special by spending it together as a threesome. A source revealed, 'Jamie has been relishing his role as daddy and it's been important to keep his two girls close at hand. They have been living close by and visiting him on set when convenient. He couldn't be prouder.'

And while it was a difficult task indeed flitting from doting dad off screen to domineering sex master on camera, Jamie seemed able to juggle the roles expertly. Moreover, playing Daddy in between takes also had the additional benefit that it put any female stars who may have been intimidated by his good looks completely at ease. Although for twenty-three-year-old singer Rita Ora, who played Jamie's adopted sister, it had the opposite effect. 'Jamie is gorgeous. And he had his wife and kid on set a lot. But that makes him hotter … an unavailable guy for me is a bit like – woohoo!'

Thanks to his good-natured and friendly co-stars and crew, with whom he immediately struck a rapport, life on set was shaping up to be good fun. As soon as Jamie had touched down in Canada and been introduced to everyone, it was clear that the cast couldn't have been better picked and bonds were quickly established. They were all there to work hard but also to have fun, and everyone got stuck into the action. 'We had a ball – a good craic. Sometimes you don't luck out with the cast – you end up with people who aren't really on your wavelength and who don't approach the game the same way but we got genuinely lucky on this,' Jamie said. 'Obviously we're getting the work done but you're allowed to have fun at work – I'd stop if I wasn't allowed to have fun.'

Filming was taking place in a variety of locations across the Canadian city, including North Shore Studios, which has played host to a string of Hollywood blockbusters as well as hit TV series *The X Files*. Additionally, the stately buildings of the University of British Columbia would provide the backdrop for college girls Anastasia and Kate's Washington State University. The impressive Bentall 5 skyscraper – the eighth tallest building in Vancouver – was used for Christian's 'Grey Enterprises' office, while the historic and flag-adorned Fairmont Hotel was used for the book's Heathman Hotel. Despite such very public film locations, everything was being done to keep the movie under wraps. Security surrounding the filming was tight with ten undercover guards reportedly hired to circle the actors and open umbrellas whenever a snapper was spotted lifting their camera to take a shot.

Despite the precautionary measures, though, sly photographs of the action on set had started to appear in newspapers and magazines across the world, including some of Jamie and Dakota dancing on the street in between takes to keep warm. The camaraderie between the pair, just two weeks into filming, was palpable. Games and japes between the two of them were a daily occurrence and included playing a street version of basketball to stave off boredom as they waited for filming to resume. 'They were very playful on set. At one point Dakota turned to Jamie and held out her hand to dance and Jamie pulled her in and put her hand on his shoulder. They weren't doing a scene they were just trying to keep warm,' an insider revealed. 'The pair would also play games, like trashketball, when you treat the trashcan as a basketball hoop. Dakota missed her shot, but Jamie made his, which caused everyone to cheer. Dakota also tried to juggle but she dropped everything and Jamie laughed at her,' they added.

It may have looked like fun and games but, behind the scenes, novice actor Jamie had his work cut out. Not only did he have thousands of lines to remember, but he had some problem areas which needed to be whipped into shape. One of these – much to his embarrassment – was his walk. Having been assigned a dance coach to teach him how to foxtrot for Christian's dance scene with Anastasia, the teacher noticed he had an odd gait. Instead of the powerful strides he needed to pull off as dynamic Christian, Jamie had a bounce to his step. This was not news to Jamie, who had been turned away from the runways in Milan when he was trying to earn a crust as a young model because of his walk.

Therefore, despite being thirty-one years old, in a bizarre turn of events Jamie was for the first time in his life being taught how to walk properly. 'I always had a complex about the way I walked and people would comment on it. I walked on my toes and when I did *The Fall* the director asked, "Is that part of the character or the way you walk?" My wife tried to help by making me lean back and then in *Fifty Shades* my character has to dance the foxtrot.'

In a bid to try to get Jamie moving more fluidly, the teacher suggested that the handsome star should try walking 'heel to toe', something most people learn as a toddler. In an eureka moment, Jamie was finally walking the way he should have done three decades ago. 'No one had ever told me that was how you walk!' he told TV talkshow host Graham Norton. 'Now I am applying it every day!'

And as filming started, there was more choreography in store for the star in the form of Jamie's endless – and intense – sex scenes with Dakota. Although scenes in the novel were graphic, X-rated and described as pornographic, the scriptwriters adapting it for a film audience needed to tone things down somewhat for a cinema release. So while they were determined to include flavours of Christian's hard-core sexual habits, his sensual romantic side was also going to be brought to the fore. 'Regardless of what you may think of [James's] writing, this is a modern love story, involving two complex characters, and that's what I'm interested in,' screenwriter Kelly Marcel said. 'I don't care what anybody says, there is something about Christian Grey that is old-fashioned and romantic.'

With filming underway, Jamie admitted that the movie was shaping up to be more like a romantic Mills & Boon novel than an S&M porn movie. 'When it comes to this movie, so much emphasis is on one thing [sex] whereas love is actually more important. It's a universal thing. Everyone has experienced it in some way and people forget that's what is at the heart of this film. It's the classic star-crossed lover situation that's been written about over and over down the years. Just with a modern element,' he told *The Sun*. 'Love will always be necessary to tell a story. Personally I think it's more important to focus on that than sex.'

Keen to keep E.L. James's sex-hungry fans happy, the infamous steamy sessions between Christian and Anastasia were still going to feature in the 'bonkbuster' and the screenwriters had been working round the clock to ensure that no one would be disappointed. The reworked script was incredibly detailed and written to incorporate every thrust, lick and flick of the whip to guide Jamie and Dakota through the process. It was more sex-by-numbers than unbridled passion, with every detail of a bedroom scene scrupulously written out with as much specification as possible. 'I couldn't just write "they made love",' screenwriter Kelly explained. 'I had to actually describe everything! It was really embarrassing when you're doing studio notes around the table with twelve people,' she added. 'There is going to be a lot of sex in the film. It's going to be raunchy. We are 100 per cent going there. We did go through and decide which are our favourite moments and which are not. Most of them are in there.'

Keeping as much of the novel's much-loved lines in the script was also crucial, as was ensuring that the sex scenes were played out as close to how the book's readers would have envisioned them as possible. A choreographer was also on hand to guide

Jamie through every seductive move he made on his co-star; it was undeniably the least romantic situation the married actor could have found himself in. Naked and surrounded by cameras, hot lights, sound-men, the director and a scurry of helpers – including hair and make-up assistants – it was a wonder he could lose himself in the moment at all. 'The reality is that burly men who you don't know very well are three feet from your face, which isn't usually the way you have sex,' he explained. 'Well me, anyway!'

However, Jamie's expertise, likely gained after years of performing for the camera in a variety of muscle-flexing sexual positions for advertising campaigns, was admirable. Often requiring enviable upper-body strength to hold a sensual pose or sexual position while his on-screen lover moved into place, Jamie described his performance as 'sexual acrobatics'. The key to Jamie's success in playing the kinky role seemed to be the ability to accept that this was work – a way to earn a crust – and he was there to entertain. 'It's strange work for sure. But it's still just work. I just get on with it,' he explained.

His co-star Dakota seemed to be equally turned off by performing the titillating scenes. 'It definitely wasn't a romantic situation. It's more like technical and choreographed and more of a task!' she explained. 'It's [less about having sex and] more about visually what our bodies look like in what we're doing, so it's more like a dance, it's like acrobatics.'

The results, however, were staggeringly convincing and powerfully sexy to all those witnessing the two actors in motion. E.L. James, sitting on the sidelines and watching Jamie act out her once-secret fantasies in front of her eyes, was also clearly impressed. Denying the red-hot passionate scenes had been axed from the movie, she said, '[The sex] is happening. Oh yeah it's happening. The bit I was seeing, it wasn't being watered down and so that's all I'll say about that!'

Talented Jamie was also an expert in 'acting out' the more unusual lines in the book including the line by Anastasia: 'Mmmm ... he's soft and hard at once, like steel encased in velvet, surprisingly tasty, salty and smooth. He's my own Christian Grey-flavoured popsicle.' Scriptwriter Marcel said, '"You are my popsicle". That line went in, it's genius. They apparently did that scene great. Apparently Jamie is great at being soft and hard at the same time. Which is hard to do for an actor! He's going to get an Oscar!'

The sex scenes weren't without risk, and balancing, thrusting, curling and whipping left Jamie riddled with bruises all over his body. 'I made sure we stuck to the book. I was a walking bruise. It was a lot of fun and I've had time to heal,' he said some weeks after filming finished.

The intense three-month production had been fast and furious, and with whispers that the star could win a host of accolades for his performance, Jamie was stunned by how differently the public and press were treating him when he finally came up for air once filming was over. It was hard to fathom that just six months previously he could have walked down the road virtually unrecognised, yet now photographers and fans were trailing him. It was certainly going to take some getting used to. 'The whole thing's ridiculous. It's just all a bit silly the way it works. I think I could lose my mind,' he said a few short weeks after filming wrapped up.

Having flown back to his cosy London town house with his wife and baby, he was then determined to have some normal family time before filming began in Belfast on the second series of *The Fall*. Although he had experienced the life of a top-notch high-flying actor with all the glitz and glamour of being on a multimillion-dollar film set, Jamie was determined to remain grounded. 'You can become a conceited a***hole or do something good in the world, the latter being much more difficult. I don't try to be cool or trendy. I'm an individualist. Mostly in life, I want to be myself,' he told Polish *Glamour* magazine.

Jamie was determined to carry on as normal and snaps of him walking around London enjoying his rare time off, sometimes with Amelia and their baby by his side, were appearing in glossy magazines and gossip blogs on a near weekly basis. Devoted fans were also starting to appear at red-carpet events, desperate to get close to Jamie and chanting his name in a bid to get his attention. Even his contemporaries within the modelling industry had him on a pedestal, as young models heralded him as a true example.

Following his extraordinary move, Jamie's rise to fame from clothes horse to world-famous actor meant that others wanted to crack Hollywood too. Renowned model and rugby player Thom Evans said, 'What would my dream role be? It sounds cringe but probably Mr Darcy.

'Jamie Dornan is a role model. I want to follow in his footsteps.'

While Jamie had ended the year on a high as 2013's best

Breakthrough Actor in a Radio Times poll, further glory was his when Jamie scooped his first ever award.

In fact, the Irish star was honoured not just once but twice at the Irish Film and Television Awards (IFTAs) in April 2014 with two awards: Best Actor for his portrayal of the murderous psychopath in the BBC drama *The Fall* and Best Rising Star.

Jamie was stunned by his double triumph and incredibly grateful. He thanked Allan Cubitt for taking a risk and casting him in the lead role – branding it 'the best professional thing that has ever happened to me' – but also his wife 'Milly' and daughter 'sleeping upstairs', who made him truly happy. As he beamed with pride in front of the cream of Ireland's TV and film industry, he said, 'I want to thank my beautiful family for being really beautiful. I want to thank my wife Milly for being the best thing that ever happened to me. I want to thank my baby who is four months old and she's sleeping right now upstairs, she's beautiful too. And I want to thank everyone who's ever met me and who's been nice to me.'

When a BAFTA nomination followed a few months later, along with winning *GQ* magazine's Breakthrough Award for his role in *Fifty Shades*, Jamie was rightly proud of his achievements. His hard work and years of endless, fruitless auditions had paid off. At last Jamie knew that ignoring the naysayers had been the right decision: ditching his profitable modelling career for acting had been worth it. 'It's special when you get that recognition especially if you feel you've taken a risk and changed direction in your career. When you're known for one thing and move into another area it's difficult initially.

'It excites me, makes me feel like I made the right decision and life is very good at the moment, I definitely can't complain.'

It had been a 'mad year, professionally and personally' for Jamie and returning to Belfast after the whirlwind of *Fifty Shades of Grey* for the second series of *The Fall* 'felt like coming home, in the loveliest way'. However, having endured six months of sleepless nights as a new dad, along with shedding all thoughts of Christian Grey to climb inside the challenging and very dark headspace of Paul Spector, had left Jamie exhausted. 'I'm tired, very tired,' he admitted, 'but very happy. It's all good. I'm glad to be back.'

It was now time to look to the future and one thing he was sure of: after playing Christian Grey, with his passion for consensual S&M, and Paul Spector, who liked to throttle his victims, a role which didn't involve ropes and tying knots would be ideal. 'There are a couple of classic knots I know now and I've put them to good use far too many times recently. In fact I'd like a job where I don't have to tie women to beds,' he joked.

The future looked rosy for Jamie and as well as enjoying some well-earned rest, the star was now eagerly and nervously waiting for the public's reaction to the release of *Fifty Shades of Grey*. A sneak preview had already been delivered in the form of a sizzling two-minute trailer released in July, with huge fanfare in the press and a range of reaction from tens of thousands of fans. The steamy video featured the moment Mr Grey – with Jamie oozing sex appeal in an immaculately tailored grey suit – meets Anastasia. Innocent Dakota was seen going for an interview in his lavish offices before the viewer was treated to a few sex-

and-bondage scenes, including the gorgeous actor pushing the brunette seductively up against an elevator wall, flying a helicopter and showing off his six-pack when crawling across a bed. The trailer ended with Anastasia naked, blindfolded and being whipped. Deemed too saucy to appear in full on American TV, it became the most popular trailer of the year with a staggering 36 million hits in its first week. Within minutes of being released online, the internet was flooded with reaction by the book's fans, along with videos of people filming themselves watching the clip for the first time. Many fans, delighted by the first sizzling glimpse of kinky billionaire Christian and college student Anastasia, took to social media site Twitter to express their excitement. 'I don't know how many times I've watched the trailer for 50 shades of grey … Omg too freaking EXCITED' @ WeeDimps said.

The book's author was also rejoicing. When fans tweeted Erika to say that they were cheering and dancing as they watched the trailer, she replied, 'Me too! Others were impressed with singer Beyoncé's slow rendition of her 2003 hit 'Crazy in Love', which accompanied the trailer. 'The only cool thing about that 50 shades of grey movie coming out is Beyonce's new version of crazy in love' @CaeMcKenna tweeted, while others were totally underwhelmed by its release, with American comedian Warren Holstein writing, 'Could we all agree on a safe word for I don't want to talk about 50 Shades of Grey?'

Some corners of the press were also panning the movie, claiming it was set to be a disaster. 'The two-minute "teaser" for the movie *Fifty Shades Of Grey*, starring Jamie Dornan, has received a public flogging after it was released this week,' critic Amanda Platell claimed. 'However bad it may be, what baffles me is why the film is already being trailed at all when it's not in cinemas until February 14 next year. It gives a whole new meaning to foreplay.'

The *Mail on Sunday* was just as scornful. 'Jamie and Dakota look depressingly clean and pretty gloomy as the saucy couple, Christian Grey and Anastasia Steele. But what the trailer does demonstrate is that the source for *Fifty Shades of Grey*, with its innocent, slightly scruffy girl and her billionaire lover, is actually Cinderella. And also that the most effective sex aid might be a helicopter,' it read. There was, however, some evidence that the trailer had delivered the desired effect on the great British public. Within an hour of the trailer being released, kinky underwear store Ann Summers saw a whopping 55 per cent surge in web traffic. Over 500 pairs of handcuffs had been bought – twice as many as the week before – along with twice the number of eye masks and triple the usual number of restraints; also, sales of diamanté whips were up 80 per cent. With over six months to go before the film's release, it was impossible to tell whether it would be a roaring box-office success or a colossal disappointment; either way something was certain: it would undoubtedly change Jamie's life forever.

Always cautious that his acting work could dry up at any time and knowing there were no certainties in life, Jamie was careful not to make any assumptions about his future as a world-famous star. 'Right now I don't need to work if there's nothing that I want to do. I've done three jobs back-to-back. Let's see how they are received. If there's nothing I want to do, I'll just play golf and change nappies,' the exhausted thirty-two-year-old said. Somehow, with a Hollywood role in his back pocket, a clutch of awards, a devoted wife and a beautiful baby daughter, it is highly unlikely that his thousands of fans across the world will let him slip into anonymity now that they've finally discovered him. But then again, a young doctor's son from Holywood with a faraway fancy of a life as an actor could dare to dream, couldn't he? Amongst the highs, the lows, the good, the bad, and the very many shades in between … if you're Jamie Dornan, it turns out then yes you can.